Game & Fish Cuisine

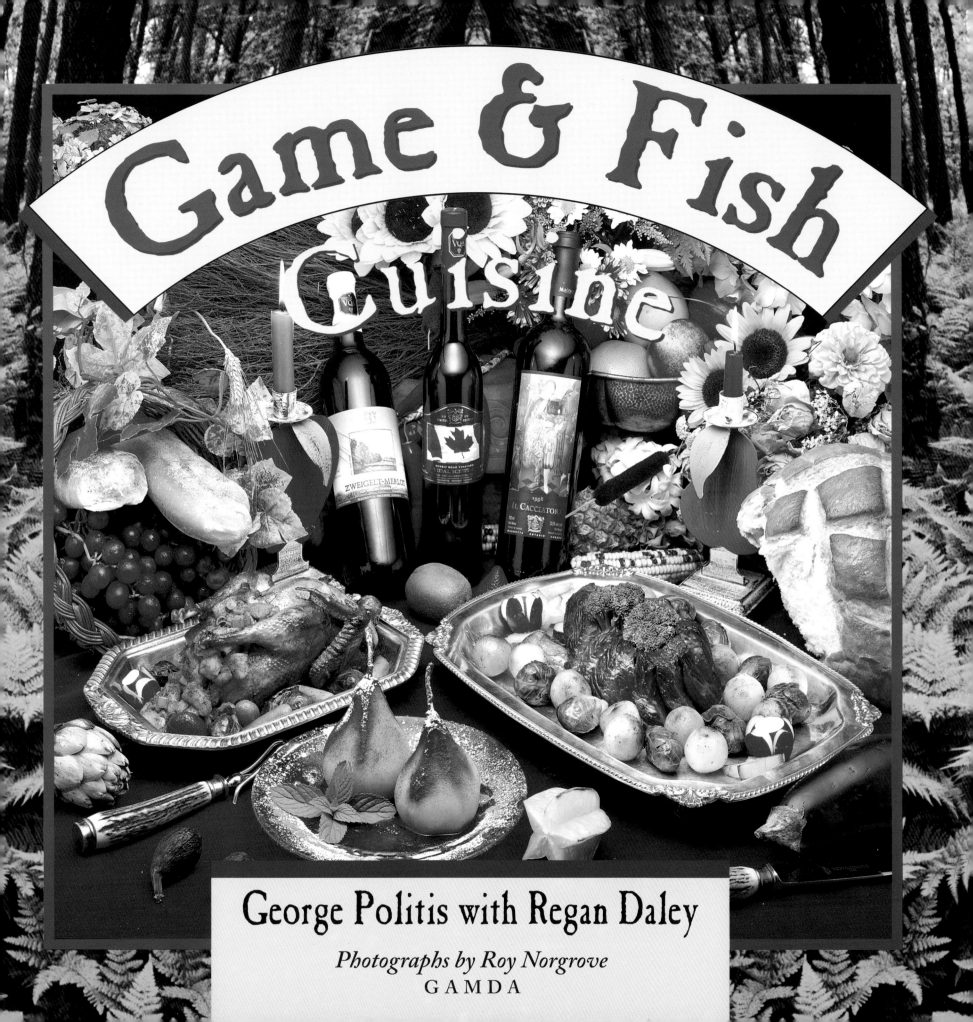

Game & Fish Cuisine

George Politis with Regan Daley

Photographs by Roy Norgrove

GAMDA

Cataloguing-in-Publication Data
Politis, George
Game & Fish Cuisine
Earlier ed. Published under title: Wild Game Cuisine.
Includes bibliographical references and index.
1.Cookery (Game) 2. Cookery (Fish) I Wild Game Cuisine.
II Title. III Title: Game & Fish Cuisine.
TX751.P648 2001   641.6'9   C2001-902141-0

GAMDA

Published by
GAMDA INTERNATIONAL CORPORATION,
44 Whitbread Ave., Bolton, Ontario Canada L7E 1L7

Food Styling by George Politis
Design by Fortunato Design Inc.

Printed and bound in Hong Kong, China
by Book Art Inc., Toronto.

❧ Contents ❧

Most people only know Gabe and Rossana by their award-winning, blue bottle Icewines. May this book of game and fish recipes serve to introduce you to their affinity for the outdoors and to their love of the inherent flavors of nature's bounty. Perhaps then you'll know Gabe and Rossana a little better and what their commitment to quality truly means.

For more than a decade since they founded Magnotta Winery, Gabe and Rossana Magnotta have shared a unique commitment to quality. It's a commitment, not just to the quality of their wines as borne out by the honor of being Canada's most award-winning winery...by far, but also to the quality of life that should be the birthright of all humanity today and on into the future. It's that commitment to the quality of life that has made them passionate proponents of conservation, active in numerous local and national initiatives from the protection and preservation of our natural wetlands to the safeguarding of our growing number of endangered species, all in addition to supporting international efforts to curb the depletion of the world's non-renewable resources.

www.magnotta.com

Magnotta Poached Pears

A real great desert that is easy to make. I really enjoy fruit prepared with sweet sauces served with a 1999 Vidal Limited Edition Icewine from Magnotta. Mmmmmm!

3 cups water

1/2 cup granulated sugar

1 tbsp lemon juice

4 almost ripe pears (bosc or others with stems on)

Caramel Sauce (optional)

1 tbsp Icing sugar

1 tbsp ground cinnamon

In a large saucepan, combine water, sugar and lemon juice. Bring to a boil over medium-high heat. 2. Peel and core pears leaving the stems in tact. Add pears to boiling syrup; reduce heat to simmer gently. Cover pot with a lid over syrup to help cook pears. Simmer for 15 to 20 minutes until tender. Remember to turn the pears halfway through cooking. 3. Pour hot caramel sauce over pears and powder with a combination of icing sugar and ground cinnamon. Makes 4 servings.

Magnotta selection 1999 Vidal Limited Edition Icewine

Dedication

For Roy Norgrove, an excellent photographer and business man, a professional who allowed me to prepare and style all of the dishes for this book and without whose glorious images, I would need a million more words.

To my spouse Toni and my three darling children, Anette, Maria and Demetre, for giving me the support and inspiration to continue this project. To my father Demetre, for finding me that first cooking job in London, Ontario; and to Karol and Wayne Latta, for providing and entrusting me with all of their beautiful materials and props that were used to style each photograph.

And finally, to all of the game farmers and suppliers who work so hard to provide the rest of us with such bounty today and in the future.

Acknowledgments

I am indebted to the Ministry of Agriculture & Food, game suppliers, and specialty grocers. Many thanks to Denise Schon for so carefully crafting a rough manuscript into such a fine finished product. To Regan Daley for the words that refined my own vision; and to Rossana and Gabe Magnotta whose dedication for game and fish cuisine is seen in the wine selections throughout the book. I am also grateful to Jules Beauregard of Hushion House Publishing and Fortunato Aglialoro, my designer, whose patient and faithful guidance allowed me to provide yet another cookbook to food enthusiasts who desire to explore nature's wildest bounty.

Preface

Food culture has expanded on an unprecedented scale since my last book *Wild Game Cuisine* was published in 1996. In North America in particular the cooking and eating of game meats accompanied by the right wine selection has become a prestigious pastime, and a hobby of the aficionados of fine cuisine.

This boom in food culture has naturally had a tremendous effect on demand and while researching *Game & Fish Cuisine* it was not uncommon to hear suppliers of free ranging farm raised game meats admit to the large back-orders for the supply and demand of this very important food sector.

Despite the change of pace forced by the great boom in their industry, game meat suppliers have contributed generously to my cookbooks for the second time.

In this new cookbook the much needed wine selections from Rossana and Gabe Magnotta combined with their enthusiasm and praise for *Game & Fish Cuisine* make this a very special reference book for food connoisseurs willing to explore the ultimate culinary experience with game meats, fish and wines.

I came by my love of wild game cooking and my passion for the wilderness naturally. From as far back as I can remember, I have spent every spare moment outdoors, completely awed by Nature and our connection to her; respect and love for the land were part of my Greek heritage. I remember watching as my uncles and brother-in-law readied themselves for a hunt or fishing trip, then as they returned with their quarry: a plump pheasant or a basket full of golden speckled trout. I was mystified. I can still recall the vibrant flavors of the meals that followed. Eventually, I accompanied them and began to understand their innate respect for the Earth, the seasons and indeed the creatures who were their prey. I became a devoted weekend hunter, honing my skills over the years as an outdoorsman as well as a naturalist.

About the same time as I was falling in love with the wild, I was being seduced by cooking. My father had a lot of connections in the community of London, Ontario, where I grew up, and when I was 15 years old, he secured me a job as a dishwasher at the Rendezvous Restaurant. I was a quick study and was soon promoted to the glamorous position of short-order cook. In spite of the modesty of the establishment, I was learning the basics of food preparation, and I became very busy experimenting at home! I later landed a job at a large hotel in town, under a chef who had worked in some of the finest hotels in Europe and the Middle East. As luck would have it, his specialty was the cooking of wild game. With his expertise to draw on in the evenings and a freezer perpetually full of all manner of wild game meats at home, my experimenting became more polished, and what was to be a lifelong love affair with wild game cooking was Firmly established. I have indulged both my passion for game hunting and cooking on my travels all over the world and have decided to compile my favorite recipes.

North Americans have entered a unique age: all around us, we see the result of several hundred years of casual disregard for our land and its inhabitants, both flora and fauna. We hear the nutrition experts condemning the genetically engineered species we have created; we hear the culinary talents complaining that much of the food we eat has lost its flavor. In the midst of this wasteland, there are ranchers and farmers raising free-range and organically fed species of wild game. These animals are the result of concern for preserving the land and the diversity of life that it sustains, as well as the desire for exquisite, nutritious food to sustain us.

There was a time in the history of our culture when humans were directly dependent on species of wild fowl, big game and fish for their survival. For hundreds of years, the native Americans shared their lives and their lands with the bison, which provided them with meat and milk for food, skins for clothing and shelter, bone and horn for weapons and basic tools. The people treated the animal with reverence, gratitude and respect. Then came the dawn of the industrial age. Suddenly, humanity's perception of its place in the world became precariously unbalanced: Man dominated Beast, and creatures that were once sacred to humans were gradually replaced with chemically engineered and hormone-enhanced "products" to satisfy our unreasonable demands for quantity and consistency. In his book *Game Birds*, Mr. Charles Cole, Director of Game Conservancy in Great Britain, writes: "We owe a great debt to our ancestors who shot, hunted and fished, for they created the warm intimate countryside that is now at risk from the agrochemicals, machines, drainage schemes, commercial afforestation and other forms of land use, which are not always [as] sympathetic to wildlife as they could afford to be." Mr. Cole is perhaps generous. In fact, we have systematically devastated great areas of wilderness and the animals they supported. Many people are awakening to the realization that the animals we have so carefully produced are inferior, rather than superior, species, with few of the nutritional virtues of their wild relatives and little or no taste! The average North American consumes many more times the amount of meat than is necessary for the body to be healthy, and the meat is usually extremely high in fat and cholesterol. Wild or free-range game animals, by comparison, are very lean and have fed on natural vitamin- and mineral-rich plants, grasses and grains. They are allowed to develop and behave naturally, running, scavenging, flying and feeding, and are raised with a minimum of human or chemical intervention. This natural existence results in lean, athletic animals with incomparable depth of flavor. The rich, delicate, slightly chewy flesh of a guinea fowl or fat little quail; the strong, gamey taste of a lean wild rabbit; the dark, forward richness of loin of venison or caribou — these complexities of flavor are inherent in the meat of game animals but completely lacking in commercially raised poultry and meat.

This book is not only for hunters. It was written to enable people to explore the rich and rewarding realm of wild game cooking. In so doing, I hope more people will become aware of our collective culinary heritage and our debt to, and relationship with, these marvelous creatures. The considerable spectrum of game animals available to the food lover today can lead us toward a more ancient and healthy diet, one in which a portion of meat is received with gratitude and respect for the animal and consumed in moderate quantities, as is anything worth savoring. If we can extend this respect and understanding to all the creatures we rely on, directly or indirectly, we can become balanced and more humble in we can again our perception of our place in nature. As we relearn what we have forgotten-to look to the seasons and the natural balance of life in nature for cues to our diet -we cannot help becoming more closely tied to this world and less alienated from the very Earth that must always support us.

George Politis
May 2001

❧ Introduction ❧

The art of wild game cooking is not rocket science, although it may seem every bit as foreign and complex. Many of my guests who enjoyed the dishes I prepared would bemoan the fact that they could not eat like that more often. They assured me that they were not qualified, that they hadn't the professional expertise or equipment necessary to prepare these seemingly exotic dishes. For a moment, I contemplated keeping this secret to myself but decided instead to write a cookbook that was targeted to the average person who is eager to explore the world of game cuisine. I do not have a fabulously equipped is kitchen or possess a diploma or degree in Haute Cuisine. I live in a big city, have a more-than-fulltime day job, and my residence is the upper flat of a house. My kitchen is 12′ x 12′ square, and my storage and preparation space is very limited. You don't need fancy equipment, exotic ingredients or years of professional training to prepare a sumptuous meal with any of these wonderful meats. Wild and free-range farm-raised game animals have a wonderful texture and unique, rich flavor that are incomparable to those of the mass-produced meats we have become accustomed to. They need only the freshest, simplest foods as accompaniments, as well as an understanding of their individual properties in cooking.

Another argument I hear is that game animals are not easily acquired. While truly wild meats are rarely sold to the consumer, most of the animals in these recipes are being raised on ranches and farms all over the continent. Game animals, often raised free-range under conditions that are as close as possible to their natural environment, approach their wild relatives in flavor and texture. Markets and farmers' markets often carry game birds and meats in season, and specialty-food stores and good butchers can usually order game products with a little advance notice. For those who do not have access to these sources, there are a number of commendable mail-order companies that supply game birds and meats to cooks all over North America. A partial list of these suppliers is included at the back of this book. With any source, do a little research. Make sure the supplier or shop can tell you everything you want to know: the age of the animal, where it is from, whether it is wild or farm-raised and whether or not it is free-range or organic. The recipes in this book are intended to be simple and flexible. If you haven't got access to the particular animal specified, consult the Quick Reference Substitution Chart on page 10, and simply adjust the cooking time according to the replacement's size.

It is the lucky cook who knows a generous hunter. If you do happen to acquire a wild game bird, rabbit or cut of big game meat, consult a reliable hunter's manual or wild meat preparation guide for information about the cleaning, hanging and aging process that is necessary. Game that is obtained from a hunter directly from the wild will taste somewhat richer and more strongly "gamey" than farm-raised animals. For some, this wild or gamey flavor is an acquired taste; for others, it is an essential part of the wonderful character of wild game animals. It varies greatly with the age of the animal: the older an animal, the more acute this taste. The gaminess of wild game can be muted with prolonged marinating (*see page 4*) and long, slow cooking. Domestic and farm-raised species are much less gamey but still have a great deal more character and complex-

Braised Grouse with Mushrooms see pp. 46–47

ity than commercially raised meat and poultry.

Unlike the commercially raised meat, poultry and fish to which we have become accustomed, game species are intensely and uniquely flavorful on their own! While most gourmets would not dream of sitting down to a plate of unadorned, unsauced, unseasoned chicken, the same cannot be said for a delicate partridge breast or a juicy morsel of quail. Many other cookbooks give detailed directions for constructing exotic dishes of game meats with rare, expensive and trendy ingredients from every culture and cuisine under the sun, but in some ways, that complexity undermines what is so refreshing and distinct about these meats. In the recipes that follow, they are paired with simple, complementary ingredients that don't overpower or mask the delicate nuances of flavor but, rather, support and enhance them. This is cooking the way it was done for centuries — indeed, some of these recipes may date back at least that far — using fresh, good-quality produce, simple and long-tested techniques and the very best meats that are available.

With the growing concern about fat consumption and diet in North America, game meats are gaining popularity for health reasons. Wild and freerange game is high in protein, vitamins and minerals and extremely low in fat. It is important to be aware of this inherent leanness when preparing game birds, rabbit or big game meats. To avoid ending up with a tough and dry piece of meat, care must be taken to ensure there is adequate moisture in the dish. The sections on Marinating, Barding and Cooking Methods will elaborate on these techniques.

Throughout the book, I have suggested accompaniments to the dishes, but they are just a few of the many possibilities! Look to the season and the flavor of the main dish when deciding what to pair it with. Vegetables in season are always the tastiest, but don't limit your choices to vegetables. Fresh seasonal fruit, dried fruit and nuts are centuries-old accompaniments for wild game, and their sweet richness balances the delicate flavors in the meats perfectly. With an autumn roast pheasant, look to other rich foods of the season — chestnuts, potatoes, baked squash, beans, root vegetables, apples, cabbage, walnuts, cranberries…. The possibilities are endless and will create a new dish each time it is served.

Garnishing your plates simply and thoughtfully will lend a professional touch to your meals. Most game dishes are spectacular when presented at the table before being carved or portioned, much like the platters presented at feasts and banquets hundreds of years ago. A golden roast goose on a platter surrounded by new potatoes and Brussels sprouts, or a dozen crisp skinned quail with lemon wedges and parsley, makes a grand statement and is actually less work for the cook than garnishing and serving individual plates. Garnishes can accent the dish with color, such as bright glazed carrots on a platter of pale rabbit, and can transform it from the simple to the sophisticated.

Once you have exposed your palate to the delights of plump, succulent game birds, rich wild duck, sweet racks of venison, delicate rabbit and the juicy, flaking flesh of brown trout and have seen how easy they are to prepare, your meals may never be the same!

Tenderizing, Hanging and Aging Wild Game

To make the flesh supple and edible for our pampered human jaws, all wild game and some large domestic animals, such as beef, must be tenderized. There are several ways to tenderize: hanging and aging, usually performed by the butcher or processor or the experienced hunter; and pounding and marinating, which can both be done at home.

Hanging and aging meats is a process that goes back thousands of years, since humans first learned to cook the meat of their prey. The effect of hanging and aging is to allow the naturally occurring enzymes in the meat to break down the tough, tight fibers, making the meat tender. The flavor of the meat is also affected: the aging produces a stronger, richer flavor.

While tenderizing isn't necessary for domestic poultry such as chicken and turkey, hanging and aging is applied to domestic beef, and in fact, well-aged beef is highly valued.

In the traditional British school of butchery, fowl are hung in feather and undrawn (uneviscerated). Hare and wild rabbit are furred and left with the entrails intact, and deer and wild boar are gutted and bled prior to hanging. The American process involves removing everything from the cavity of the animal immediately after slaughter, and it is skinned or its feathers removed. Often it is tenderized by a combination of hanging, aging and freezing.

With all big game, some form of hanging and aging is required. Wild game birds and rabbits, especially older, tougher animals, may be hung by the feet for a short time. Any game that is available retail, be it wild or farm-raised, will already have been hung for market, if hanging was needed. If you find yourself in possession of a wild animal that has not been processed at all, consult a reference book or butcher before proceeding with any technique.

The tenderizing process can be furthered at home by mechanical or chemical methods. With mechanical methods, the fibers of the meat are physically broken down by pounding with a wooden or metal tenderizing mallet or by grinding the meat.

Chemical tenderizing involves introducing an enzyme to break down the fibers, such as the enzyme papain in commercial meat-tenderizing powder or the acid in a marinade *(see section on marinades, page 4)*.

❧ Marinades ❧

Marinades are seasoned liquids, usually containing an acid in the form of wine, vinegar or lemon juice, that flavor and tenderize meat. The word "marinate" derives from the Spanish word meaning "to Pickle," or "mere." The acid helps break down tough fibers, and the meat absorbs the flavors of the seasonings used. The ingredients can vary widely—virtually any flavor can be incorporated into a marinade. Marinades may be raw, as is the case with the following easy-to-prepare recipes, or cooked.

Choose glass, stainless-steel or ceramic containers to hold marinades, and wooden or stainless-steel implements for whisking and stirring. Aluminum and copper can taint the marinade and meat with objec-tionable flavors and odors, because the acid in the marinade reacts with the metal.

If part or all of the marinade is to be used in a recipe, strain out the solids and discard before pro-ceeding.

For each of the following recipes, whisk together the liquids in a nonreactive container until emulsified, then add the remaining ingredients. Refrigerate, cov-ered, until needed, up to 2 weeks. Marinate meat for 3 to 4 hours minimum or, ideally, 24 to 48 hours. Game birds should be rinsed and dried before marinating; some, such as quail, should be checked to ensure they have been properly eviscerated—no organs should remain inside the cavity.

Marinade for Game Birds

1 cup olive oil

1 cup dry white wine

Juice of 3 lemons

2 sprigs fresh rosemary

2 branches fresh oregano

Whisk olive oil, wine and lemon juice together to form an emulsion. Add the herbs, and refrigerate until needed, up to 2 weeks.

Variations: If a strong lemon flavor is not desired, replace part or all of the lemon Juice with additional white wine.

Herbs may be varied to suit the recipe: substitute thyme, parsley, sage, tarragon or basil.

Marinade for Waterfowl

2 cups dry red wine

$1/4$ cup soy sauce

Juice & zest of 1 orange

$1/2$ cup extra-virgin olive oil

2 sprigs fresh tarragon

2 bay leaves

Whisk together wine, soy sauce, orange juice and zest. Slowly add to olive oil, whisking constantly. Add tar-ragon and bay leaves, and refrigerate until needed, up to 2 weeks.

Variations: Soy sauce and/or orange juice maybe omitted for a more neutral flavor. Increase the quanti-ty of wine in these cases.

Tarragon may be replaced with any other fresh herb.

Marinade for Small Game

1 cup olive oil

¾ cup dry red wine

½ cup port

2 celery stalks, coarsely chopped

2 small onions, peeled & finely chopped

2 fresh parsley stalks

2 bay leaves

2 tsp. crushed black peppercorns

2 sprigs thyme

Whisk together olive oil, wine and port until emulsified. Add remaining ingredients, and refrigerate until needed, up to 2 weeks.

Variations: The quantities of port and red wine may be adjusted in favor of one or the other, as long as the total amount is about 1¼ cup.

White wine may be used in place of port-red wine combination

Thyme may be replaced with any other fresh herb, such as tarragon or rosemary.

Marinade for Big Game

2 ½ cups dry red wine

1 cup olive oil

Juice of 2 lemons

2 stalks celery, coarsely chopped

3 stalks fresh parsley

2 sprigs fresh thyme

2 bay leaves

1-2 Tbsp. crushed black peppercorns

Whisk together red wine, olive oil and lemon juice. Add remaining ingredients, and refrigerate until needed, up to 2 weeks.

Variations: Replace all or part of the lemon juice with red wine vinegar (about 4 cup total).

Vary the herbs used according to the recipe: substitute rosemary, tarragon, sage, basil, etcetera.

Sauces

The following are four of the infinite number of sauces that accent and enhance game meats. A sauce should complement the flavors of a dish but should never be used to mask a poorly cooked or flavorless one. Nor should a sauce overwhelm the dish; rather, it should support the nuances of flavor in the meat.

Soubise Sauce

This is a simple variation of a classic, versatile sauce. Delicate and mild, soubise sauce is wonderful with all types of roast or poached fowl or with simple fish or vegetable dishes.

4 cups peeled, finely sliced white onions

3 cups milk (not low-fat)

$^3/_4$ cup 35% (whipping) cream

$^1/_2$ tsp. salt

$^1/_8$ tsp. ground white pepper

In a heavy medium saucepan, cover sliced onions with 2 cups of the milk. Slowly bring to a boil, then reduce the heat, and simmer until onions are very tender. Strain, reserving the onions, and return the milk to the saucepan. Add the cream and remaining I cup milk, and simmer again until reduced by half. Meanwhile, purée the onions in a food processor or food mill, and return to the saucepan with the milk-cream mixture. Stir over medium heat until the sauce is homogenous and thick enough to coat the back of a wooden spoon. Season to taste with salt and white pepper, and serve warm.

Pâté de Foie Gras Sauce

This sauce is a luxurious accompaniment to game birds and accents rather than disguises the richness of their flavor. Serve it at room temperature on the side of the dish.

8 oz. package cream cheese (not reduced-fat), softened

$^1/_4$-$^3/_4$ cup 35% (whipping) cream

2 tsp. Madeira or port

2 $^1/_2$-3 oz. pâté de foie gras (fresh or tinned)

In a medium bowl, beat cream cheese, adding the 35% cream a tablespoon at a time until the mixture is smooth and loose. In a separate bowl, blend the Madeira into the pâté to form a smooth paste. Add this mixture to the cream cheese mixture, and beat together until thoroughly combined.

A Tip: When serving Fois Gras on its own, try an exquisite Ontario Icewine for a match truly made in heaven.

Orange-Cranberry Sauce

Most people know this festive sauce as the traditional accompaniment to holiday roast turkey or chicken. Its fresh, bright tang complements all varieties of game birds and many big game meats, such as wild boar.

1 lb. fresh cranberries

$1/2$ cup freshly squeezed orange juice

$1/4$ cup port

2 cups firmly packed brown sugar

Grated zest of 1 orange

$1/8$ tsp. salt

Wash and pick over the cranberries. Combine all ingredients in a heavy-bottomed, nonreactive saucepan, and place over low heat. Stir constantly until the sugar is melted, then raise the heat, and bring the mixture to a gentle simmer. Cook until all the cranberries have popped open, about 10 to 12 minutes. Transfer sauce to a clean container, and cool. Sauce may be refrigerated until needed, up to I month, and served warm or cool.

George's Tomato Sauce

This is a versatile and flexible sauce. I like to make it fresh as often as possible, but it freezes very well, and can be made in large batches, so there's always some on hand! Feel free to use your favorite vegetables. When tomatoes are in season, I use fresh ones; otherwise, good-quality canned tomatoes are a fine substitute.

3 lbs. fresh ripe tomatoes, or one 28 oz. can peeled

whole or crushed plum tomatoes

4 Tbsp. olive oil

1 onion, peeled and finely chopped

3 cloves garlic, peeled and minced

1 green or red pepper, seeded and chopped

1 tsp. chopped fresh oregano

1-2 cups any other appropriate vegetable desired

(mushrooms, zucchini, eggplant, etc.), chopped

Salt and freshly ground pepper, to taste

2 Tbsp. fresh basil, in fine strips

(optional, in season)

1. Peel the fresh tomatoes, if using: cut out the stem of each tomato, and make a small cross in the other end with a sharp paring knife. Bring a pot of water to boil, and blanch the tomatoes for 30 seconds to 1 minute, depending on the ripeness. Remove them from the water, and plunge immediately into a bowl of ice water to stop the cooking. The skins should slip off easily. Scoop out the seeds, and chop the tomatoes. If using canned tomatoes, chop roughly.

2. In a large non-reactive saucepan, heat the olive oil over low heat. Add the onion and garlic, and cook until softened, about 3 minutes. Add tomatoes, peppers, oregano, and any other vegetables desired, and raise heat to medium-low. Simmer partially covered for 10 to 15 minutes, or until sauce is thickened and vegetables are soft. Stir occasionally, and take care not to scorch the sauce. Season to taste with salt and pepper, and add the basil. If sauce is to be frozen, do not add basil, but wait until sauce is defrosted and ready to serve, as the herb will lose much of its flavor by freezing.

❧ Game and Wine ❧

Not long after the first human being discovered that the flesh of animals was much better cooked over a flame than it was raw, someone else, to whom we are forever indebted, coupled this meat with wine, and dinner was born. The perfect combination of game meat and wine can enhance each element and create a taste experience more wonderful than either one alone. Today, the once hard-and-fast rules about how to pair wine and food have expanded to the point where the phrase "red wine with meat, white wine with poultry and fish" is virtually obsolete. The light and dark meat categories themselves are challenged by game meats: many game birds, correctly called poultry, have only rich, dark meat and would overpower a wine that may be ideal with domestic poultry. Similarly, while the white flesh of domestic rabbit is mild and delicate, wild rabbit and hare have intensely flavored dark meat.

First and foremost, you must drink wines you like. If you do not enjoy drinking red wine, then go ahead and drink a good, full-bodied white with venison. If your tastes are somewhat more flexible, then there are a few basic things to consider when choosing a wine. Always match the wine to the strongest flavor in the dish. With most domestic meats, that will be a sauce or garnish, but with wild game, the most remarkable flavor is frequently the meat. Fortunately, game meats and wine are natural partners. Both exhibit, in the best cases, great depth and complexity of flavor and reflect in taste and texture or body their *terroire*, or native environment. When choosing a wine, it is often helpful to look to the region from whence the dish originates — a wine from that region will have many of the same nuances of flavor. If a wine has been used in the preparation of a dish, the wine consumed at the meal should be of a similar type. Finally, when considering wine as a partner to wild game, the degree of complexity must be balanced. Complexity is found in finer, more mature vintages, in good wines that have been aged to develop depth, body and character. This is not to say that every meal of wild game must be accompanied with an expensive bottle of wine! Many of the dishes in this book are wonderful with a good, hearty table wine, but there is no finer meal to serve with a top-quality wine than one of wild game.

The following recommendations are intended to be guidelines and are meant to steer the curious diner toward some of the possible marriages. With all species of game, the wild variety will be more intense and strongly flavored than the farm-raised or domestic and will demand a more complex and aggressive wine.

Light and Dark Meat Game Birds, Wild and Domestic

Roasted: This elegant dish can support the finest wines, both white and red. For whites, a full-bodied, dry Chardonnay or a crisp Alsatian-style Pinot Gris. For dishes accompanied by fruit sauces or compotes, a dry Riesling would be appropriate. An alternative is any fine mature red: Burgundy, Bordeaux, New World Pinot Noir, or Cabernet Sauvignon.

Braise, Stew or Casserole: Generally a dish for reds, but a full-bodied dry white will stand up to it. Try a Fumé or Sauvignon Blanc or a full-bodied Ontario Chardonnay. A complex and full-bodied red in the burgundian or bordelaise style balances the flavors well.

Dark Meat Game Birds, Wild and Domestic

Roasted: Definitely an excuse for the best red you can afford: A fine barrel aged Cabernet Sauvignon, Merlot or Carmenère.

Braise, Stew or Casserole: A robust intense red in the style of the Southern Rhone or Barolo.

Duck and Goose

Wild: An aggressive but good-quality red, such as an Australian Shiraz, Ontario barrel-aged Maréchal Foch, or full-bodied California Zinfandel. For a white, choose one that is rich and fat-in-the — mouth, such as a good Ontario Viognier or barrel fermented Chardonnay.

Domestic: A good New World Gamay or Pinot Noir.

Rabbit and Hare

Wild Rabbit and Hare: A medium-bodied complex red, such as Ontario Meritage or Cabernet Franc.

Domestic Rabbit: A young, fruity red, such as Beaujolais or a Zweigelt Trebe. A delicate Sauvignon Blanc, Riesling, or Gewürztraminer would be a good match as well.

Big Game Meats

Venison, Caribou, Bison: Rich, mature, full-bodied reds such as Cabernet Sauvignon, Carmenère or Merlot. The rarer the meat is served, the younger the wine should be to support it. With grilled or peppery dishes, well-matured, full-bodied reds are appropriate. For those who don't appreciate very hearty reds, a good Pinot Noir is an excellent alternative.

Wild Boar, Antelope, Elk: Fine, full-bodied New World reds, with some maturity or a somewhat softer red such as a medium-bodied Ontario Merlot.

Quick Reference and Substitution Chart

Meat	Flesh Color	Flavor	Substitution
Pheasant	light / dark	mild to sweet	guinea fowl, Cornish hen
Guinea Fowl	light / dark	delicate	pheasant, Cornish hen
Partridge	pink / dark	rich	young pheasant, grouse
Grouse	light / dark, dark	delicate to strong	partridge, Cornish hen
Quail	dark pink	delicate, rich	small game birds
Cornish Hen	light / pink	mild, like chicken	chicken, guinea fowl, young pheasant
Woodcock	dark pink / dark	rich, gamey	quail
Goose	dark	rich, full	duck
Duck	dark pink	strong, rich to gamey	other waterfowl
Rabbit, domestic	light	mild, delicate	light-meat fowl
Rabbit, wild	dark	gamey, strong	hare
Hare	dark	rich, strong, gamey	wild or large domestic rabbit
Moose	dark red	rich, gamey	caribou, bison, venison
Caribou	dark	gamey, strong	moose, venison, bison
Antelope	medium dark	strong, like goat or mutton	lamb, goat, venison
Venison	dark red	rich, gamey, strong	lamb, beef, goat, bison
Bison	dark red	delicate, rich, like beef	moose, venison, beef, caribou
Elk	dark red	rich, delicate, strong	caribou, moose, venison, bison
Wild Boar	dark pink to red	rich, gamey	venison, antelope, pork

Nutritional Information

The following statistics are approximations only and should be viewed as guidelines, rather than indisputable fact. There may be slight deviations from these numbers when considering wild game, as opposed to farm-raised animals. (Sources: USDA, Composition of Foods: Raw, Processed, Prepared. Washington, D.C.: USDA, 1976 – 1993; and information provided by the food industry.)
*Statistics are based on a 3.5-ounce (100g) serving of each meat.

Meat	Calories	Protein (g)	Fat t (g)	
Chicken -with skin	200-240	25-26	7-9	
-no skin	140-145	26-27	3-4	
Pheasant -with skin	145-151	24-25	4-5	
-no skin	130-135	22-24	3-4	
Guinea Hen -no skin	108-110	19-21	2-3	
Partridge -with skin	215-220	25-27	12-14	
Grouse -with skin	215-220	25-27	12-14	
Quail -with skin	160-168	23-25	6-7	
Duck -with skin	330-340	18-21	25-30	
-no skin	195-205	20-25	10-12	
Goose -with skin	300-305	24-26	20-22	
-no skin	235-240	28-30	12-13	
Rabbit and Hare	125-175	20-22	3-5	
Beef- marbled cut	240-265	23-25	16-18	
Beef -lean meat	185-200	26-27	14-15	
Pork		219-225	23-29	11-13
Wild Deer, Caribou	125-130	20-22	3-4	
Venison, Moose	135-160	18-23	3-5	
Bison	130-140	35-36	1-3	

Game Birds

There is something eternally appealing about a perfectly roasted plump little bird — simple, humble and mouth-watering! Whether it is a bevy of crisp-skinned quail or a single fat pheasant, a meal of game birds will be as unforgettable as one of chicken is ordinary. Until recently, enjoying the delicacy of wild game birds was the exclusive indulgence of successful hunters. In recent years, however, the number of types of game birds available to food lovers who may not hunt at all has risen immensely. Farms all over North America, many of them organic, are raising both domestic and wild species of pheasant, quail grouse, guinea hen, duck, goose and others for sale through butchers and specialty-food sources. A taste of one of these wonderfully flavorful birds might make you think twice before choosing a steroid-enhanced chicken again!

Upland and Woodland Birds

Wild game birds fall naturally into two groups: upland and woodland birds, and water and marsh fowl. Upland and woodland birds include the pheasant, guinea hen, grouse, partridge, woodcock and quail. They nest in the high grasses of the prairies, the dense woodland of forests or the sandy underbrush of the plains. They are smaller than the average chicken and very different in constitution. Wild species of game birds have very lean flesh and little or no protective fat. Game birds, in spite of their wings, spend most of their lives scurrying about on foot, relying on their agility and camouflage, rather than flight, to protect them. They use their wings only to overcome obstacles or to cover great distances quickly. As a result, the legs and thighs of upland and woodland birds are much denser and more muscular than those of a chicken. To illustrate the difference, compare the legs

Previous page: Roast Wild Goose, see page 72

of a person who does no exercise with those of a marathon runner. To achieve a juicy, succulent result, the cook must compensate for this leanness by introducing some form of moisture to the bird during cooking. Barding with bacon or salt pork is a traditional way to roast game birds, and in some cases, the fat can be replaced with thick leaves, such as grapevine leaves *(see the section on Barding on page 22)*. Many dishes call for the birds to be marinated before cooking *(see page 4)*, and any wild or older birds should be marinated regardless of what the recipe says. Many of the following game birds can be substituted for one another; check the Quick Reference Chart on page 10 for the best alternatives, and adjust the cooking time according to the size of the bird.

Pheasant

Originally a native of Asia, the pheasant was introduced to Greece by Roman traders and endeared itself so well that it ultimately made its way to the wilds of Europe and North America. For hundreds of years, the pheasant was revered in Europe for what was perceived as a noble character along with its supreme delicacy. Indeed, it may be the most divine and best-loved game bird for the gourmet. Today, they are raised on farms all over North America and are sold at three weights: 1-pound, or young, pheasants; 2-to-2$\frac{1}{2}$-pound adults; and 3-to-4-pound mature birds. Buy the adult weight if possible; mature birds are significantly tougher and must be braised, and young pheasants are hard to find and very expensive. There is a significant difference in flavor and texture between the wild and farm-raised pheasant: wild birds have a much more pronounced gamey flavor and darker, leaner meat. Domestic pheasant are delicate, mild-tasting and usually moister and plumper. Females are preferable, because their flesh is less muscular and more tender than that of males. If possible, buy from free-range suppliers: the meat will be laced with the flavors of the scavenged food, such as nuts and seeds, and will be closer in flavor to that of the wild bird.

Guinea Fowl

Guinea fowl, also called guinea hen, originated on the west coast of Africa but is now plentiful in the same regions of the world as the pheasant. In fact, it is very similar to pheasant in flavor and texture, with moist, slightly chewy meat. Guinea fowl have quite a large frame, with little fat and a high ratio of bone to flesh so the yield of meat is lower than one might expect for its size. Wild guinea fowl are smaller, on average, than their domestic cousins, which range from about 1 to 4 pounds. As with all game birds, the more tender, younger birds are preferable. Guinea fowl are very lean, and barding is recommended when roasting. For wild guinea fowl or domestic birds over 2½ pounds, barding is essential. Small birds may be marinated and grilled or roasted, and large or older hens should be braised.

Quail

A golden, crisp-skinned quail perched on a mound of buttery mashed potatoes may be one of the simplest and most delicious dishes in history! The quail is indigenous to North America, Asia, Europe and Australia and is perhaps the game bird most widely available to consumers. Even domestic quail are tender,

dense and flavorful, and the wild birds are gamey in taste. Quail are lean and must be barded before roasting. They also benefit from marinating and fast cooking, such as grilling or pan-frying. Regardless of the method of cooking, the breast should remain pink, and care must be taken not to overcook the little birds. Most recipes call for quail to be left whole: indeed, they used to be eaten in one bite with the fingers. Selective breeding has resulted in a larger bird, called jumbo quail. Quail can be purchased at anywhere from 5 to 8 ounces. Plan on serving two large quail a person as an entrée or one each for an appetizer or salad portion.

Partridge and Grouse

These two game birds are very closely related and, in some regions, are often confused. The two most common species of partridge that live wild in North America are the chukar, native to the Himalayas, and the Hungarian partridge, introduced to this continent for sport hunting in the last century. In fact, there are dozens of species available to the hunter today, and more and more are being raised to benefit the food lover. Grouse is also plentiful in numerous varieties in North America and Europe. Wild birds of both types are hunted throughout the fall months until early December. The flavor of partridge and grouse is actually more closely related to their diet and environment than to the particular species. Wild birds will be more strongly gamey and extremely lean. Farm-raised fowl are delicately flavored and rich, with slightly chewy, dense meat. There are subtle differences between them, however. Partridge have meatier legs, and grouse have proportionately larger breasts. The flesh of wild grouse is somewhat darker than that of partridge, and the legs, unless of a very young bird, are too tough for anything but braising or stewing. Because both birds are very lean, they should be barded when roasted and marinated whenever possible.

Cornish Game Hen

The Rock Cornish game hen is not a wild bird at all but the delicious result of a cross between a Cornish game-cock and a Plymouth Rock hen. Very easy to find commercially, they are a less costly alternative to game birds. Fed on a diet that often includes acorns and cranberries, they are more flavorful than chicken but not as strong as wild fowl. Their almost completely white meat is juicy and tender and very forgiving to cook. They may be used in most of the recipes in this section but do not need barding or basting with additional fat.

Woodcock

This plump little game bird is available only to the hunter and to any fortunate friends who happen to be nearby. Its dark, chewy meat is similar to that of quail, and it can have a slightly livery taste, depending on its diet. The recipe I have included for woodcock can easily be made with large quail or small grouse and is Just as good.

Marsh Fowl and Waterfowl

To even the most urban of North Americans, the wild duck and goose are strong, eternal symbols. Pilgrimages of majestic Canada geese herald the end of summer and the dawn of fall, and deep in winter, holiday celebrations are centered around golden roast birds: perhaps a goose for Thanksgiving or a brace of ducks at a Christmas feast. The cooking of waterfowl and marsh fowl has a special place in my heart, and my passion for them is shared by many. With no other bird, however, is the distinction between wild and domestic so clear. The taste of a lean, rich wild duck or goose is incomparable to the often oily, greasy, flavorless taste of their domestic counterparts. There are nuances in flavor in individual species, as in birds from different environments — the lakes, marshes, fields of grain, corn and peas all find a way into the flavor and contribute to the richness and complexity of wild waterfowl. Over my years of both hunting and cooking, the mallard has become my ultimate favorite, thanks to its intense flavor and rich, dense meat. Free-range farm-raised wild species of duck and goose can be delicious and tasty in their own right but are, as the saying goes, just not the same. You can narrow the gap with both birds by treating the domestic fowl with understanding: the greatest difference is the proportion of fat on the farm-raised birds. While wild waterfowl are athletic and very lean, much like wild upland and woodland birds, domestic ducks and geese have a thick layer of fat covering their dense, lean flesh. This fat, if left unrendered, will prevent the bird from crisping, browning and cooking properly and will make the meat oily and unpleasant. Follow the simple directions on page 19 to render this fat, and the domestic bird can be cooked much the same as the wild one, rewarding you with delicious results.

Duck

Contrary to popular belief, the dark, juicy flesh of wild ducks-and domestic ones beneath the fat-is relatively low in both fat and cholesterol, so it need not be avoided by the health-conscious. (I have enjoyed roasted wild duck with several physicians, and they have agreed, especially after being swept away by the taste!) The most urgent concern when cooking wild or rendered duck is to avoid overcooking. Duck is best when roasted to medium-rare so that the juices of a pierced thigh run pink. If cooked to the same degree as chicken, duck's succulent and tender flesh becomes tough. Wild ducks should be well marinated and/or barded before roasting and are wonderful when slowly braised or used in soups and stews. Young duck is excellent when marinated and grilled; the turn-of-the-century writer Alexander Innes Shand hailed it as "the jewel of the spit." Duck breasts may be removed and sautéed or grilled, the denser legs reserved for braising *(see page 25 for instructions on how to remove the breasts)*. If you are purchasing a domestic duck, buy

what appears to be the leanest and do render the fat. Mallards are smaller than most domestic ducks, at about 3 pounds, but look for farm-raised birds of about 4 to 7 pounds. This size will feed two to three people.

Goose

As with duck, there is a world of difference between the wild goose and its farm-raised cousin. With a great deal of active flight, wild birds remain very lean, while mostly sedentary domestic waterfowl become very heavy with fat. Buying a free-range bird will minimize this difference, but the bird won't have the same depth of flavor that a wild one would. Domestic geese, however, are far from lacking culinary attributes. If the fat is properly rendered *(see page 19)*, free-range geese are rich, delicate and wonderfully juicy, with hints of apples and young onions in the flavor. Young birds are best: an 8-to10-pound goose feeds about four to six people and will still be tender and succulent. The definitive way to cook a goose, wild or domestic, is to roast it. Golden and rich, with luxurious juices, a perfectly roasted goose is a triumph of flavor! Goose should be thoroughly cooked, unlike duck, and the juices should run very pale yellow when a breast is pricked.

❧ Cooking Methods for Game Birds ❧

Game birds may be cooked in a number of different ways, depending on the leanness of the meat, the age of the bird and the part of the bird being cooked. Younger, more tender birds that have a higher fat content or have been marinated or barded may be cooked using dry methods of cooking, such as roasting, grilling or broiling and sautéing or frying. Older birds, or those that are very lean, benefit from moist methods, such as braising and stewing.

Dry methods of cooking

Roasting

Roasting is one of the simplest and finest ways to enjoy the flavorful flesh of game birds. The very image of a beautifully roasted bird, crisp-skinned and golden, evokes anticipation and hunger in even the most stoic of diners! Roasting is best for young and tender birds. An added source of fat is needed for most game birds, such as barding with bacon or salt pork *(see Barding, page 22)*. With careful vigilance, barding can be replaced in some cases with rubbing with fat, such as butter or oil, before roasting, then basting frequently.

An alternative to barding with fat is to wrap the bird in several layers of moistened grapevine or cabbage leaves. This method works very well with small game birds, such as quail. With this technique, however, the flesh actually steams, rather than roasts, and the result will be quite different from the classic roast. The skin will not become crisp and golden, and the flesh may be slightly less dense. The birds may be browned in olive oil before wrapping, or the skins rubbed with a little olive oil. Soak the grapevine or other leaves in warm water and wine, if desired. Wrap the leaves around the birds, and secure them with string.

Jus, gravies and sauces

Some recipes call for the fat to be skimmed from the cooking juices in the roasting pan, and other ingredients, usually thickeners, to be added to make a gravy. Other recipes leave the jus clear and thin, to be spooned over the meat and accompanying vegetables. Either method is wonderful, and even when a recipe does not stipulate what to do with this liquid, use it! It contains incredibly rich flavor, and even the simplest gravy makes a good roast great. The skimmed liquid can be thickened with a little cornstarch paste (cornstarch blended to a smooth paste with a few tablespoons of cool water) or with a few tablespoons of extra-fine flour. Seasonings, herbs, a little dash of Worcestershire sauce, orange juice, wine, brandy or other liquid flavoring may be added. Bring the liquid to a gentle boil, and whisk until suitably thick.

Grilling

One of the oldest cooking methods, grilling has recently become very fashionable, thanks to its inherent healthfulness. Birds may be grilled over a bed of hot coals or open fire, or they can be turned on a spit. Grilling is a dry method of cooking, best suited to young, moist or marinated meat and quick cooking. Broiling under the oven broiler simply inverts the process, with the heat coming from above rather than below the meat.

Sautéing and pan-frying

Although sautéing and pan-frying use hot fat as a cooking medium, they are considered dry methods of cooking. The meat, either a small whole bird or pieces of bird, is cooked quickly over high heat to caramelize the skin and seat in the juices and flavor.

Moist cooking methods

Braising

Braising begins with some of the same techniques as sautéing: use high initial heat, and fry in fat to sear the outside of the bird, then add a small amount of liquid, and cook longer at a lower temperature. The liquid adds moistness to the dish, making this method appropriate for leaner, tougher or older birds. The dish may be partially or completely covered during cooking.

Stewing

With stewing, a large proportion of liquid is used, and the cooking of the meat takes place in the heated broth. Vegetables and other seasonings are added to flavor the meat and the broth. The cooking liquid is sometimes left thin and served before or along with the meat, or it can be reduced or thickened, becoming a sauce for the bird. Stewing is most appropriate for very lean, tough or old birds but can be used for any bird with delicious results.

Rendering fat from a domestic duck or goose

Unlike their wild counterparts, domestically raised ducks and geese have a thick layer of fat under the skin. Left intact, this fat makes an otherwise lean and healthy meat highly calorie and prevents the proper cooking, crisping and browning of the birds, By steaming the birds for a short time before proceeding with the recipe, the fat can be rendered and the bird treated much more like its free-flying cousins.

Prick the skin of the bird in several places with a sharp knife. Take care not to puncture the flesh underneath. Place the bird on a small rack set in a roasting pan or large pot, and add enough water to come just below the rack but not touching the bird. On the stove, bring the water to a boll, then reduce to a simmer, and cover the pan. Steam for 30 minutes, then proceed with the desired recipe.

The highly flavored fat rendered is valued by many gourmets for adding to soups and stews, and it makes the most heavenly sautéed potatoes! It can be refrigerated and melted as needed.

❧ Trussing Game Birds ❧

Trussing a bird is done to ensure that all parts of the bird cook evenly. It may be done with string, pins or skewers and involves tying the wings and legs securely to the body so that no part of the bird protrudes from the uniform, compact shape.

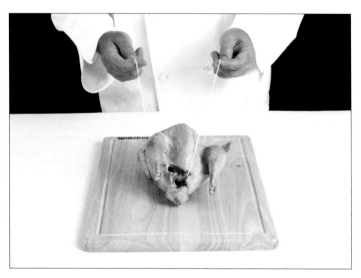

1. Place the bird on its back, with the legs pointing away from you. Cut a piece of cotton kitchen string about three times as long as the bird. Bring the center of the string up under the little knob of cartilage and skin called the parson's nose.

2. Tie a simple knot over the parson's nose, then bring the ends of the string toward you, between the legs and breasts. Cross the strings in front of you, tucking them under the stub of the neck.

3. Pull the ends of the string back around the bird by taking them beside the breast again but winding around the leg knuckle instead of meeting at the parson's nose.

4. Wrap the string around the knuckles several times, binding the legs close to the body of the bird. Turn the bird over, and secure the string in place with a bow knot. Place the bird on its back again, and tuck the wing tips under the breasts. The bird is trussed and ready for roasting.

❧ To Roast a Game Bird ❧

1. Preheat oven to 350°F Pat the bird dry, and season inside the cavity and all over the skin with salt and pepper. Pull the skin from the neck and breast tight, and secure it under the bird with a small, thin skewer.

2. Rub the skin of the breasts, legs, thighs and wings with olive oil. Truss the bird, and place in a roasting pan, then into the oven.

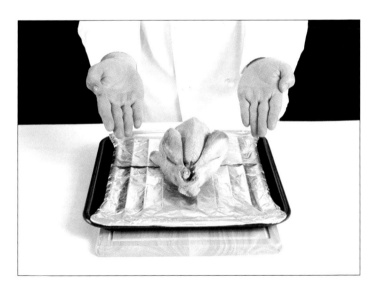

3. Roast, basting frequently, until the bird is tender and golden. Allow roasted bird to rest for 15 to 20 minutes before Serving.

✌ Barding Game Birds ✌

When game birds and wild ducks and geese are roasted, some type of barding material should be used to compensate for their leanness and to insulate the breasts from overdrying. A quail roasted without fat is tough, stringy and dry, but when barded with a few strips of bacon, it comes out succulent and Juicy. Thin slices of salt pork or bacon are excellent for barding.

1. Barding is placed over the trussed bird and tucked into the space between the thighs and legs.

2. Additional strips are then laid over the breast and tucked around the wings.

3. Finally, the barding material is secured onto the bird with cotton string.

❧ Disjointing Game Birds ❧

Although the prospect of disjointing a bird into serving pieces may be daunting, it is a very simple technique. Today, most of us buy poultry pieces under plastic wrap, already butchered, and have little need for knowing how to do it ourselves. Disjointed game bird pieces are useful for preparing stews and casseroles or for sautéing quickly. In addition, different parts of the bird may be used for different preparations: tender breasts may be grilled, while the legs and wings are saved for creating a tasty stew.

Halving a Game Bird

1. With poultry shears or a sharp knife, cut along both sides of the backbone, and remove it.

2. Keeping the bird on its back, turn it around so that the legs are pointing toward you. Using the heel of a heavy knife, cut through the white cartilage of the breastbone with one strong whack.

3. Continue the cut until the two sides of the bird are cleanly divided, removing any stray bits of cartilage or bone.

Disjointing Game Birds

Cutting a Bird Into 4, 8 or 9 Pieces

1. Follow the instructions above for halving a game bird. Beginning with one half, cut through the loose skin between the leg and the breast. When you meet resistance, bend the leg outward, exposing the Joint, and cut through it. Repeat for the other half. Breasts may be left on the bone or removed. You now have a bird in 4 pieces.

2. For 8 serving pieces from a large bird, each breast may be cut in half, and the thigh separated from the drumstick. For a smaller bird, breasts and legs should be left whole. Wings may be removed, and the carcass may be cut into several pieces for ease of use in stocks and soups, creating a total of 9 Pieces, with 6 serving pieces including 2 wings.

Internal Temperature Chart for Game Birds

For the most accurate test of doneness, use an instant-read meat thermometer. This method is more reliable with game birds than the traditional "minutes-per-pound" rule, since the density of the flesh of game birds differs so much from that of domestic chicken and turkey. Internal temperature should be taken with an instant-read meat thermometer inserted at the thickest part of the breast or the inner part of the thigh. The bulb of the thermometer should not touch the bone.

Chicken	180°F-185°F
Pheasant, Guinea Fowl, Quail, Grouse, Partridge	160°F-170°F, *or until juices ran pale pink when thigh or underside is pierced*
Cornish Game Hen	175°F-180°F
Goose	165°F-170°F
Duck	155°F-160°F

❧ Disjointing Game Birds ❧

Removing Boneless Breasts From a Wild Duck (or other large game bird)

1. Place the bird breast side up on a cutting surface. With a large knife, cut between the back and breast sections, severing them completely. Set aside the legs and wings for another use.

2. Place the breasts skin side up on the board, and pull the skin tight with one hand. Feel for the breastbone, and insert the tip of a thin, sharp knife immediately against it on one side. Follow this cut along the breastbone, then retrace it, deepening the cut until the breast comes away from the bone. Repeat on the other side.

3. Pull the skin off the breasts, using the knife just to sever the fine membranes, letting your fingers do most of the work.

4. You now have two lovely fillets of duck breast.

Lemon Pheasant

I was first introduced to this dish when I was 16 years old while visiting my parent's home village in the Kalamata region of southern Greece. While not quite as famous as the local olives, this recipe is the favorite way of preparing pheasant.

1 2-to-2½-lb. pheasant
Salt & freshly ground pepper
1 cup dry white wine
Juice of 2 lemons
2 Tbsp. chopped fresh oregano
¼ cup extra-virgin olive oil

1 Preheat oven to 375°F. Wash pheasant, and pat dry. Season well with salt and pepper, truss *(see page 20)*, and place in a roasting pan just large enough to hold it comfortably. In a mixing bowl, whisk together wine, lemon juice, oregano and half the olive oil until the mixture is emulsified. Rub the pheasant thoroughly with this marinade, and let stand at room temperature for 15 minutes.

2 Pour the remaining oil over the bird, season with salt and pepper, and add a little water to the roasting pan. Cover and place the pan on the middle rack of the oven. After 45 minutes, remove the cover, and continue roasting, basting frequently, for 30 to 45 minutes, or until the juices of a pierced thigh run pale pink and the skin is golden. This dish is excellent with roast potatoes and, for a very Greek touch, rice as well!

Makes 4 to 6 servings 11.

Variation: *Tarragon Roast Pheasant*
Omit oregano, and combine 3 tablespoons chopped fresh tarragon with salt and pepper. Rub the pheasant well with this mixture after pouring the remaining oil over the bird, and garnish with fresh tarragon sprigs.

Magnotta selection Ducks Unlimited 1999 Viognier VQA

Rosemary Pheasant with Wine

My wife and I fell in love with this dish at a romantic little French bistro in Québec. To be appreciated properly, it should be shared between lovers.

1 2-to-21/2-lb. pheasant, split in half *(see Halving a Game Bird, p. 23)*
Salt & freshly ground pepper
3 Tbsp. butter
1/4 cup olive oil
3 Tbsp. chopped fresh rosemary
2 Tbsp. cornstarch
1 cup dry white wine
5-8 large white mushrooms, sliced
$\frac{1}{2}$ lb. young French green beans, the thinnest you can rind

1 Preheat oven to 350°F. Wash and dry the pheasant thoroughly, and season with salt and pepper. In a large skillet, heat 1 tablespoon of the butter with 2 tablespoons of the olive oil over medium-high heat. When the foam from the butter subsides, brown the pheasant halves on both sides, beginning with the skin side.

2 Place halves side by side in a shallow roasting dish, cover with foil, and roast for 45 minutes. Remove cover, baste with the pan juices, and sprinkle with chopped rosemary. Reduce oven temperature to 325°, and continue roasting for 45 minutes to 1 hour, until skin is golden and the Juices of a pierced thigh run pale pink. Let pheasant rest on a warm platter, covered with foil, for 15 minutes.

3 Meanwhile, drain off excess fat from roasting pan, reserving the natural Juices. In a small bowl, combine cornstarch with a small amount of wine, stirring until smooth. Add cornstarch mixture and the remaining wine to roasting pan, place over high heat, and whisk constantly until sauce becomes thickened and smooth. Set aside, and keep warm.

4 In a medium sauté pan, heat the remaining butter and oil over medium heat. Sauté mushrooms and green beans together until beans are just tender. To serve, pour sauce over pheasant and surround with mushrooms and green beans.

Makes 4 to 6 servings.

Magnotta selection: 1998 Blanc Fume' Gran Riserva

Smoked Pheasant with Wine

Smoking is an ancient way of preserving meat, used extensively before modern cold storage was available, and is still a wonderful treatment of pheasant. This dish makes a quick, easy and unusual weekday meal. A Magnotta Fumé Blanc would be a perfect match.

4 medium boiling potatoes

2 Tbsp. butter

2 Tbsp. extra-virgin olive oil

2 medium cooking onions, peeled, halved & thinly sliced

1 tsp. chopped fresh oregano

2 sprigs fresh rosemary

Salt & freshly ground pepper

1 smoked pheasant, skin removed, quartered *(see p. 24)*

1 In a small pot, boil potatoes in salted water until just tender, but not overcooked. Drain and cool slightly. Peel potatoes, and slice into 1/2″-thick medallions; set aside.

2 In a large skillet, melt butter with olive oil over medium heat, add onions, and sauté until they soften, about 5 minutes. Add potato slices, raise heat slightly, and cook, stirring occasionally, until potatoes begin to brown on both sides. Stir gently to avoid crushing the potatoes. Add the oregano and rosemary sprigs, and cook together for 2 minutes, until aromatic. Remove from heat, and season with salt and pepper.

3 To serve, place pheasant quarters on a serving platter, and surround with onion-potato mixture.

Makes 4 servings.

Pheasant Paprika

Hungarian cuisine has as many variations of Chicken Paprika as there are Hungarian cooks! This is one I devised to use a wild pheasant — the spice gives the roast a gorgeous deep color.

1 2-to-2¹⁄₂-lb. pheasant, quartered *(see p. 24)*

2 cups all-purpose flour

Salt & freshly ground black pepper

2 Tbsp. butter

2 Tbsp. olive oil

2 Tbsp. Hungarian paprika

¹⁄₂ cup homemade chicken stock, or canned low-salt broth

1 Preheat to 400°F. Wash pheasant pieces, and pat dry with a paper towel. Place flour and salt and pepper in a strong plastic bag, and add pheasant pieces, two at a time, shaking to coat thoroughly. Shake off excess. Melt butter and oil together in a large skillet over medium-high heat. When foam subsides, add pheasant pieces skin side down, turning after about 4 minutes to brown both sides. Remove pheasant to a baking dish just large enough to hold pieces in one layer, and sprinkle with paprika.

2 Add the stock to the skillet, and deglaze over high heat, scraping up any brown bits. Pour this liquid over the pheasant pieces, cover with foil, and place on the middle rack of the oven for 30 minutes. Remove foil, reduce temperature to 350°, and continue baking for another 20 to 30 minutes. The pheasant should be golden, and the juices of a pierced thigh should run pate pink. Serve with mashed potatoes and steamed broccoli or spinach.

Makes 4 servings.

Roasted Pheasant with Soubise Sauce

In classical French cuisine, a soubise sauce is a luxurious creamy onion sauce, often served with poultry or eggs. Here, it accents the delicate flavor of roast pheasant and creates a dish that has become a Thanksgiving tradition in my house.

16 pearl onions

1 2-to-2$^1/_2$-lb. pheasant

Salt & freshly ground pepper

4 thin slices salt pork or bacon

$^1/_4$ cup butter

8-12 button mushroom caps

1 recipe Soubise Sauce *(see p. 6)*

1 Bring a small pot of water to a boil, add pearl onions, and blanch for 1 to 2 minutes. Remove onions, and plunge into a bowl of ice water to stop the cooking. Slip the skins off carefully, and set the onions aside.

2 Preheat oven to 375°F. Wash and pat dry pheasant, and season with salt and pepper. Lay slices of salt pork or bacon over breasts and legs, and truss bird, tying slices in place in the process. Place pheasant on a rack in a roasting pan, and roast, uncovered, for 1$^1/_2$ to 1$^3/_4$ hours, or until the juices of a pierced thigh run pale pink. Baste at 20-minute intervals during the final hour.

3 Meanwhile, in a small saucepan, sauté the pearl onions in the butter over medium-low heat, until soft and beginning to color, about 10 minutes. Add the mushroom caps, sauté 2 minutes, and set aside, keeping warm.

4 To serve, place pheasant on a warmed platter, and surround with the pearl onions and mushrooms. Pour some of the Soubise Sauce over pheasant, and pass the rest in a sauceboat.

Makes 4 to 6 servings.

Magnotta selection: 1999 Assemblage VQA (a blend of Riesling, Pinot Gris and Gewürztraminer)

Guinea Fowl with Chestnut Stuffing

The late fall brings not only a glorious bounty of game birds but also some classic accompaniments, such as chestnuts. Fresh chestnuts are a little finicky to peel, but their nutty, mild flavor is well worth the effort.

$^1\!/_2$ lb. fresh chestnuts

2 Tbsp. olive oil

3 Tbsp. butter

1 medium onion, finely chopped

$^3\!/_4$ cup dry bread crumbs

$^1\!/_4$ cup brandy

1 Tbsp. chopped fresh parsley

1 2-to-3-lb. guinea fowl

Salt & freshly ground pepper

1 To prepare chestnuts: Bring a small pot of water to a boil. With a small, sharp knife, make a cross in the skin of each chestnut. Add them to the boiling water, and boil until the skin is splitting and the fruit is tender. Some may be done sooner than others, so check frequently. When all are done, drain and set aside until just cool enough to handle (if chestnuts are too cool, they will be very difficult to peel). With the aid of a paring knife, peel off the skins, and cut chestnuts into quarters. (Chestnuts may be prepared up to 2 days ahead.)

2 Preheat oven to 375°F. In a medium saucepan, heat olive oil and 1 tablespoon of the butter over medium-low heat. Add onions, and sweat until soft and lightly colored, then add bread crumbs, chestnuts, salt and pepper to taste and brandy.

Cook, stirring, until crumbs are moistened and all ingredients are thoroughly combined. Remove from heat, add parsley, and let cool.

3 Season guinea fowl with salt and pepper, and rub the skin with the remaining 2 tablespoons of the butter. Spoon stuffing into the cavity, making sure not to pack it too tightly, as this could result in the splitting of the bird during roasting. Truss bird, and place in a roasting pan just large enough to hold it. Roast, covered, for 1 hour. Uncover, baste with the pan juices, and roast for a further 30 to 45 minutes, or until the juices run clear when the underside is pricked with a fork. Serve with roast squash and a buttery Chardonnay.

Makes 4 to 6 servings.

Roast Guinea Fowl with Apples

The delicious flavor of guinea fowl is perfectly balanced by the caramelized tartness of the apples. I try, whenever possible, to use crab apples. If crab apples are not available, use any other tart cooking apple that retains its shape well, such as Cortland.

1 2-to-3-lb. guinea fowl

Salt & freshly ground pepper

1 medium cooking onion, peeled & quartered

1 bay leaf, preferably fresh

6 crab apples, or 4 Cortland (medium-size) apples, cored but not peeled

2 Tbsp. olive oil

1/4 cup butter

1/4 cup brown sugar

1 Preheat oven to 375°F. Wash the guinea fowl, and pat dry. Season all over with salt and pepper, and place the onion and bay leaf into the cavity. Truss the hen according to instructions on page 20, set in a large roasting pan, and surround with the whole apples. Rub the skin of the bird with olive oil, and set aside.

2 In a small saucepan over low heat, melt the 60 butter. Add brown sugar, stirring just until melted together, being careful not to burn the mixture. Let cool slightly, then spoon this mixture into the cored apples.

3 Pour a little water into the bottom of the roasting pan, cover, and bake for 45 minutes. Remove cover, baste the guinea fowl with the pan juices, and cook, uncovered, for another 25 to 45 minutes, until the skin is golden and the juices run clear when the underside is pierced with a fork. Check the apples periodically to prevent overcooking: the tip of a small knife should slide in and out easily, but the apples should hold their shape. If the apples are done before the hen, remove them from the pan, and keep warm. This dish is wonderful served with roast potatoes and a fresh green salad.

Makes 4 to 6 servings.

Partridge Breasts with Wild Rice

Wild rice adds its earthy, nutty taste to the gamey flavor of partridge. Games bird have been served on pieces of toasted bread in Europe since the Middle Ages. They act as a base for the dish and are softened by all the delicious Juices. I prefer rye, but any sturdy, country-grain bread will work.

$^1/_2$ cup wild rice

$^1/_4$ cup long-grain rice, rinsed

6 boneless partridge breasts

Salt & freshly ground pepper

2 Tbsp. olive oil

2 Tbsp. butter

2 sprigs fresh rosemary

$^1/_4$ cup port

6 small slices rye or other sturdy bread

1 Cook the wild rice in $1^1/_4$ quarts boiling water for 30 minutes, or until it just begins to split. Add long-grain rice, and continue cooking until both rices are tender but still slightly chewy, about 20 to 30 minutes. Drain and reserve.

2 Meanwhile, wash breasts, and pat dry; season with salt and pepper. Heat olive oil and 1 tablespoon of the butter in a sauté pan over medium-high heat, and sauté the breasts until golden, about 3 minutes each side. Add rosemary sprigs and port, and reduce heat to medium. Cook, turning once, until breasts are cooked through. Remove breasts from the skillet, and keep warm.

3 Add the remaining tablespoon of butter and rice mixture to the sauté pan. Stir over low heat just long enough to coat and flavor the rice. Toast bread. Place one breast on each crouton, and serve immediately with scoops of the wild rice mixture.

Makes 2 to 5 servings.

Braised Partridge with Rosemary

In the grasslands of southern Saskatchewan, near the Montana border, coveys of Hungarian partridge cluster around the old abandoned homesteads of the early 20th century. I was captivated by the taste of these birds while on a hunting trip to that area some years ago, and this dish is the perfect showcase for them.

2 1-lb. partridges

2-2$^1/_2$ cups dry red wine

1$^1/_4$ cup finely chopped shallots

5 sprigs fresh rosemary

2 tsp. butter

2 tsp. olive oil

1 Prepare a marinade: In a shallow, nonreactive dish just large enough to hold partridge halves, combine wine, shallots and rosemary sprigs. Place partridge in the marinade, adding more wine if necessary to cover, and let stand for 24 hours refrigerated or 3 to 4 hours at room temperature.

2 Remove partridge from marinade, reserving liquid. In a medium to large nonreactive saucepan, heat butter and oil over medium-high heat until the butter foams. Pat breasts dry, add to the saucepan, and brown on both sides. Add the reserved marinade, reduce heat, and simmer, partially covered, for 30 minutes, or until breasts are tender. Serve with poached pearl onions and wild rice, and garnish with fresh rosemary.

Makes 2 servings; can he doubled.

Magnotta selection: 1999 Pinot Noir Special Reserve

Grouse Casserole

Richly flavored and delicious, this stew is the perfect dinner for an aprés-ski party with friends. It is almost as good when made with partridge, quail or guinea hen.

2-3 medium-size carrots, peeled

2 green onions, roots & limp ends cut off

4-5 inner celery ribs (heart)

8-10 small new potatoes, halved

2 onions, peeled & quartered, with root end intact

1 bay leaf

4 sprigs fresh parsley

1 cup chicken stock, preferably homemade, or canned low-salt broth

$^1/_4$ cup butter

2 Tbsp. olive oil

2 large or 3 small grouse, each quartered *(see p. 24)*

Salt & freshly ground pepper

2 Tbsp. chopped fresh parsley

1 In a large soup pot, combine carrots, green onions, celery, potatoes, onions, bay leaf and parsley sprigs. Add stock and enough water to barely cover. Bring to a boll, reduce the heat, and simmer until vegetables are tender. Remove all but the onions and bay leaf, cut into bite-sized pieces, and reserve.

2 Melt the butter with the oil in a large skillet over medium-high heat. Wash grouse, and pat dry; season with salt and pepper. When the foam subsides, add the grouse pieces, a few at a time, and brown on both sides. Remove from the skillet, and repeat with the remaining pieces until all are browned. Deglaze the skillet with $^1/_2$ cup of the warm stock, scraping up any brown bits from the bottom. Pour this liquid back into the soup pot along with the grouse pieces. Cover, bring to a boll, reduce heat, and simmer until grouse is very tender, about 1 hour. Return the chopped vegetables to the stew, and season to taste with salt and pepper. Sprinkle with chopped parsley, and serve with lots of crusty bread to soak up the broth.

Makes 4 to 6 servings.

Magnotta selection: 1999 Cab Franc Merlot VQA

Stuffed Roast Grouse Breasts

The breasts are the most tender part of the grouse, not quite as gamey-tasting as the legs, but subtler and complex. I had this elegant dish for the first time at a lovely country inn near Elora, Ontario. (Partridge or guinea fowl may be substituted for the grouse.)

2 large grouse breasts, with the wing bone attached

Salt & freshly ground pepper

1 Tbsp. butter

$^1/_4$ cup extra-virgin olive oil

1 medium onion, finely chopped

1 Tbsp. chopped fresh rosemary

1 Tbsp. chopped fresh thyme

1 cup dry bread crumbs

2 Tbsp. chopped fresh parsley for garnish

Fresh rosemary sprigs for garnish

1 Preheat oven to 350°F. Working on a cutting board, use a sharp, thin-bladed knife to make a slit about 1$^1/_2$″ deep in the thickest side of each breast. The slit should be just long enough to let you slip your finger into the breast, and keeping the opening as small as possible, enlarge the cavity on the inside so that it will accommodate the stuffing. Season the breasts with salt and pepper, and set aside.

2 In a small saucepan, heat butter and I tablespoon of the oil over medium-low heat. Sweat the onions until they are soft and just beginning to color. Add the rosemary and thyme, cook until the mixture becomes fragrant, then add the bread crumbs. Stir over low heat until the crumbs are thoroughly

moistened, then set aside to cool slightly. Using your ringers and a teaspoon, insert half of the stuffing into each breast, making sure they are not overstuffed and that the opening closes cleanly.

3 Rub the remaining olive oil onto the breasts, and place them in a small ovenproof dish. Cover and bake for 45 minutes. Uncover, baste the breasts with the pan juices, and return to the oven for another 30 minutes, or until the breasts are tender and the juices run clear when the breasts are pierced. Garnish with chopped parsley and fresh rosemary sprigs, and serve with buttered rice and glazed carrots.

Makes 2 servings.

Magnotta selection: 1999 Chardonnay Barrel Aged VQA

Braised Grouse with Mushrooms

This dish always reminds me of fall and the beauty of the uplands where I have hunted for as long as I can remember. Grouse has one of the most pronounced flavors of any of the game birds and brings that element of the wild to the table of even the most urban of gourmets. This dish may be made with partridge, guinea fowl or pheasant if you don't know a grouse hunter. *(See photo page x.)*

2 2-lb. large grouse, halved *(see p. 23)*

Salt & freshly ground pepper

2 Tbsp. olive oil

3 Tbsp. butter

$^1/_4$ cup Worcestershire sauce

1 large onion, finely chopped

$^1/_2$ cup chicken stock

$^1/_4$ cup water

$^1/_2$ lb. small white mushrooms, sliced

1 tsp. cornstarch

1 Preheat oven to 375°F. Wash grouse, and pat dry; season with salt and pepper. In a large roasting dish or Dutch oven, heat olive oil and 1 tablespoon of the butter over medium-high heat. Working in batches, brown the grouse halves on both sides. When all of the grouse pieces are done, set them aside, and brush with Worcestershire sauce. Drain off excess fat from the pot, and add onions. Cook, stirring, until onions are browned. Deglaze the pot with chicken stock, scraping up any brown bits from the bottom. Return grouse halves to pot, pouring in any accumulated juices, add $^1/_4$ cup water, cover, and place in the oven. After 45 minutes, remove the cover, and continue cooking until grouse is tender, about 15 to 25 minutes.

2 Meanwhile, in a medium sauté pan, melt the remaining 2 tablespoons butter over medium-high heat. When foam begins to subside, add mushrooms, and sauté until all the liquid evaporates and the mushrooms begin to brown. Remove and keep warm.

3 When grouse is tender, remove from the pot to a warmed platter. Skim off the excess fat from the liquid in the roasting pan. In a small bowl, combine cornstarch with a small amount of water to make a smooth, pourable paste, and add this, whisking constantly, to the cooking liquid. Place over high heat, and whisk until the sauce thickens. If it becomes too thick, add a small amount of water. To serve, surround the grouse halves with the sautéed mushrooms, pour the sauce over the birds, and serve with buttered carrots.

Makes 4 servings.

Magnotta selection: 1999 Pinot Noir VQA

Baked Quail with Parsleyed Rice

This superb dish was on the menu for a fundraising dinner I attended. I sneaked into the kitchen to beg the recipe from the chef and scribbled it down on a slip of paper. Over the years, I have modified it somewhat, and it has become a favorite.

6 large quail, marinated overnight in Marinade for Game Birds *(see p. 4)*

Salt & freshly ground pepper

$^1/_4$ cup olive oil

1 cup long-grain rice

2 cups water

2 Tbsp. butter

3 Tbsp. chopped fresh parsley

1 Preheat oven to 375°F. Remove quail from marinade, and pat dry. Season with salt and pepper, and truss the legs together with string. Rub quail all over with 2 tablespoons of the olive oil, and place them in a baking dish just large enough to hold them comfortably. Cover and bake for 15 minutes. Uncover, baste with the remaining olive oil, and return to the oven for another 20 to 30 minutes, or until the quail are tender, but still juicy, and the juices run pale pink when the underside is pricked with a fork.

2 Meanwhile, in the Final 20 minutes of roasting, combine rice and water in a small pot, and simmer until rice is al dente. Toss with the butter and 2 tablespoons of the chopped parsley; keep warm.

3 When quail are done, place on a platter, surrounded by the rice, and garnish with remaining parsley.

Makes 3 to 4 servings, depending on size of quail.

Magnotta selection: 1999 Chardonnay Merritt Road VQA

Grilled Quail

These juicy, smoky birds drizzled with lemon, good olive oil and fresh oregano are the essence of sunny Greek cuisine. Quail are celebrated there, and with this recipe, they'll become a favorite of yours too. Try this with any other small game bird, adjusting the grilling time according to size.

Juice of 2 lemons

$1/_2$ cup extra-virgin olive oil

2 Tbsp. chopped fresh oregano

2 Tbsp. brandy

Salt & freshly ground pepper

6 large quail, halved *(see p. 23)*

1 In a medium-size nonreactive bowl, combine lemon juice, olive oil, oregano, brandy and salt and pepper to taste. Whisk to emulsify, then add quail, turning to coat thoroughly. Marinate quail 3 to 4 hours or overnight.

2 Heat grill or broiler to high. Make sure grill bars are clean, and wipe them with a lightly oiled cloth to prevent sticking. Remove quail from marinade, reserving the liquid, and wipe off excess. Season with salt and pepper, and grill quail, skin side down, for about 5 to 6 minutes. Turn and continue cooking until nicely browned and tender about 2 to 3 minutes. Serve immediately with rice and fresh lemon wedges.

Makes 3 to 4 servings.

Braised Quail with Pasta

This is an easy, delicious dish — with a green salad and some good bread, it is as perfect for a busy weeknight as it is for a special dinner.

6 large quail, halved & marinated in Marinade for Game Birds *(see p. 4)* for 3 to 4 hours or overnight

Salt & freshly ground pepper

2 Tbsp. butter

3 Tbsp. olive oil

1 tsp. chopped fresh rosemary

1 clove garlic, minced

1 lb. fresh noodle-shaped pasta, such as fettuccine

1¹/₂ cups George's Tomato Sauce *(see p. 7)*, or a good-quality purchased sauce

1 Remove quail from marinade, wipe off excess, and season with salt and pepper. Heat butter and 2 tablespoons of the olive oil in a large skillet over medium-high heat, and brown quail on both sides. Reduce heat to medium, add rosemary and garlic, and continue cooking until quail are golden brown and tender, about 10 minutes.

2 Meanwhile, bring a large pot of salted water to a boil, add pasta, and cook until it is al dente. In another small saucepan, heat tomato sauce over low heat, taking care not to burn it. Drain pasta, and toss with the remaining 1 tablespoon olive oil. When quail are done, remove from skillet and keep warm. Add the pan drippings to the tomato sauce. To serve, spoon sauce over pasta in a large serving dish, and top with quail.

Makes 4 to 5 servings.

Baked Quail Canapé

This magnificent dish is a tribute to the rustic beauty of the North American countryside. It is an elegant and unusual opener for an intimate dinner with friends, when the snow is deep outside and the fire is bright within.

6 quail, marinated 3 to 4 hours or overnight in Marinade for Game Birds *(see p. 4)*

Salt & freshly ground pepper

2 Tbsp. olive oil

2 Tbsp. butter

$1/4$ cup water or chicken stock

6 slices dark rye, or other sturdy country-grain bread

1 Tbsp. chopped fresh parsley

1 Preheat oven to 375°F. Remove quail from marinade, wipe off excess, and season with salt and pepper. Heat oil and butter in a large skillet over medium-high heat, and brown quail quickly on all sides. Transfer to a shallow roasting pan that accommodates them in one layer, and deglaze the skillet with the water or stock. Add these drippings to the roasting pan, cover, and bake for 15 minutes. Uncover, baste, and continue cooking until quail are tender and juices run pale pink when the underside is pierced with a fork, about 10 to 15 minutes.

2 When quail are done, toast bread slices, and use a biscuit cutter or small knife to cut the bread into rounds or hexagonal shapes. To serve, place one quail on each crouton, spoon pan juices over, and sprinkle with chopped parsley.

Makes 6 first-course servings or 3 main-course servings.

Magnotta selection: 1996 Viognier Limited Edition

Fresh Pasta with Woodcock, Walnuts and Parmesan

Woodcock are wonderful gamey little birds that, unfortunately, are not available commercially yet. Do not despair: this dish, full of rich and complex flavors, may be prepared with other small game birds, such as medium-size quail or squab.

4 woodcock, or medium-size quail, marinated 3 to 4 hours or overnight in
Marinade for Game Birds *(see p. 4)*

Salt & freshly ground pepper

2 Tbsp. butter

$^1/_4$ cup olive oil

2 tsp. chopped fresh oregano

$^1/_3$ cup shelled walnut pieces

1 lb. fresh noodle-shaped pasta, such as fettuccine

$^1/_2$ cup grated Parmesan cheese

1 Remove woodcock from marinade, wipe off excess, and season with salt and pepper inside and out. In a large skillet, beat butter and 1 tablespoon of the olive oil over medium-high heat. Brown woodcock on all sides, then reduce heat, and add oregano and walnuts. Sauté, partially covered, turning the birds occasionally, until golden and tender and the juices run clear when the underside is pierced with a fork. Remove woodcock from skillet to a cutting board, and separate legs and breasts using a small knife or your ringers.

2 Meanwhile, bring a large pot of salted water to a boil, and cook pasta until it is al dente. Drain and toss with remaining olive oil. On a large serving platter, arrange woodcock pieces and pan Juices over pasta, reserving walnuts. Sprinkle with Parmesan, and top with walnuts. This dish is wonderful with garlic-rubbed bread and a dry medium bodied red wine.

Makes 4 servings.

Magnotta selection: 1999 Cabernet Franc Limited Edition VQA

Broiled Rock Cornish Game Hen

This easy recipe for these succulent little birds is wonderful any night, but especially when you haven't got a lot of time for preparation.

2 Rock Cornish game hens

$^1/_4$ cup freshly squeezed lemon juice (about 2 lemons)

$^1/_2$ cup butter, melted & cooled

1 Tbsp. freshly chopped oregano

Salt & freshly ground pepper

1 Preheat broiler. Remove the wing tips from each bird at the first joint. With a pair of poultry shears or a sharp knife, cut along either side of the backbone until they are free. Place the birds skin side down on the cutting board, and flatten them out through the breastbone with the heel of your hand. Wash and pat dry, and place the birds in a large, shallow roasting pan. Combine lemon juice, melted butter and oregano in a small bowl, and brush this mixture over the birds liberally. Season well with salt and pepper, and set aside to marinate for 15 minutes.

2 Broil for 2 to 3 minutes as close as possible to the heat, watching carefully to prevent scorching. Move the pan to the middle rack of the oven, and continue broiling, basting frequently, for about 15 minutes. Turn the birds over, baste again, and cook another 15 minutes, or until the juices of a pierced thigh run clear. Serve with rice or roast potatoes and fresh steamed summer vegetables.

Makes 2 servings; can be doubled.

Magnotta selection: 1998 Pinot Gris Special Reserve

Braised Rock Cornish Game Hen

Cornish hens are truly the most succulent of the nonwild game birds. With them, less care about marinating and barding needs to be taken, and they can be prepared in many different ways. Braising them in a flavored stock makes them even more tender and juicy.

2 Rock Cornish game hens

Salt & freshly ground pepper

1 Tbsp. olive oil

2 medium-size onions, thinly sliced

1 cup chicken stock, preferably homemade, or canned low-salt broth

1 cup dry red wine

2-3 small zucchini, sliced into $1/4''$ rounds

1 Tbsp. butter

Juice of 1 lemon

1 Preheat oven to 350°F. Season game hens with salt and pepper, truss *(see page 20)*, and set aside. In a large baking dish, heat olive oil over medium-low heat, add onions, and sweat them until they are soft and golden. Place hens on top of onions in the baking dish. Pour the stock and wine over the hens, and bring liquid to a simmer. Cover with foil, and bake for 1 to $1^1/_2$ hours, or until hens are tender and the juices run clear when a thigh is pricked with a fork.

2 Meanwhile, bring a small pot of salted water to a boil, add zucchini, and cook until crisp-tender, about 3 minutes. Drain and toss with butter and lemon juice.

3 Hens may be halved or presented whole, on top of the braised onions, accompanied by the zucchini medallions and quartered pan-fried new potatoes.

Makes 4 servings.

Breast of Duck with Walnuts

For this sophisticated entrée, be sure to use only the freshest walnuts, shelling your own, if possible. California black walnuts are rich and meaty and have a buttery, unbitter flavor that marries very well with duck.

6 boneless duck breasts, preferably wild, or farm-raised wild species, such as mallard

1 recipe Marinade for Waterfowl *(see p. 4)*

Salt & freshly ground pepper

2 Tbsp. olive oil

1 Tbsp. butter

114 lb. chopped shelled walnuts

$^1/_2$ cup dry white wine

2 Tbsp. brandy

1 Marinate duck breasts 24 hours or overnight.

2 Remove breasts from marinade, wipe off excess, and season with salt and pepper. Heat olive oil and butter in large skillet over medium-high heat, and add duck breasts, skin side down. Sauté until skin is crisp and golden, then flip breasts, and cook on the flesh side until they are medium-rare and tender. Set aside and keep warm.

3 In the same skillet, stir walnuts with the pan drippings over medium-low heat, until they are fragrant and hot, taking care not to burn them. Add wine, and increase heat. Reduce by half, scraping up the brown bits from the bottom of the pan, then add brandy. Return the duck breasts to the skillet for a minute to coat them with the walnut jus, then arrange on a platter cloaked by the sauce. Serve immediately with roast potatoes and steamed green beans.

Makes 4 servings.

Roast Wild Duck with Wild Rice

This is a spectacular dish for a large dinner party. If wild duck is not available, try to purchase farm-raised duck of a wild species, such as the noble mallard. The remarkable flavor will be worth the effort!

3 wild ducks, or farm-raised wild species, such as mallards

Salt & freshly ground pepper

3 small onions, peeled & quartered

3 bay leaves

3 Tbsp. butter

3 Tbsp. olive oil

$\frac{1}{2}$ cup dry red wine

$\frac{1}{2}$ cup + 2 cups water

2 cups homemade chicken stock, or canned low-salt broth

1 cup wild rice

1 cup long-grain rice

$\frac{1}{3}$ cup brandy

1 If using domestic ducks, follow instructions on page 19 for rendering the fat. Preheat oven to 400°F. Wash ducks, and pat dry; season well with salt and pepper. Insert a quartered onion and a bay leaf into the cavity of each bird, and truss *(see page 20)*. Heat butter and olive oil together in a large skillet, and sauté ducks, one at a time, over medium-high heat, until well browned. Place the ducks side by side on a rack in a large roasting pan, and pour red wine and $\frac{1}{2}$ cup water into the bottom of the pan. Cover and roast for 45 minutes, basting frequently. Uncover and continue cooking until ducks are tender and the Juice of a pierced breast runs pink, about 30 minutes more.

2 Meanwhile, combine the remaining 2 cups water, chicken stock and wild rice in a medium saucepan. Bring to a boll, and simmer until rice jus begins to split. At this point, add the long-grain rice and simmer until both rices are tender but still chewy. Add the brandy to the saucepan during the last 5 minutes of simmering; season rice with salt and pepper to taste. Place ducks on a large serving platter, and serve surrounded with the flavored rice.

Makes 8 servings.

Magnotta selection: 1999 Cabernet Sauvignon VQA

Roast Duck with Grapes

The grape harvests all over the world coincide with the beginning of crisp fall and the start of the hunt. Grapes have been a favored accompaniment to game birds for hundreds of years.

1 wild duck, or farm-raised wild species, such as mallard
(see p. 19 for how to render fat from a domestic duck)

Salt & freshly ground pepper

1 medium onion, peeled & quartered

1 bay leaf

2 Tbsp. olive oil

1 Tbsp. butter

$^1/_2$ cup water

$^1/_2$ lb. red grapes, plus additional for garnish

$^1/_2$ cup dry red wine

1 tsp. cornstarch

Fresh watercress for garnish

1 Preheat oven to 375°F. Pat duck dry, season wet] with salt and pepper, insert onions and bay leaf in the cavity, and truss bird *(see page 20).* In a large skillet, heat the oil and butter over medium-high heat, and brown duck on all sides. Transfer to a rack set in roasting pan, and add about $^1/_2$ cup water. Reserve the skillet and pan drippings. Cover the duck, and bake for 1 hour, basting occasionally. Uncover and roast for another 45 minutes, basting frequently, until the juices of a pierced breast run pale pink.

2 Meanwhile, add grapes to the skillet, and sauté over medium heat until grapes begin to split. Add wine, deglazing the skillet by scraping up any brown bits, and reduce the wine by about half.

Remove a few tablespoons of liquid, and combine with the cornstarch to make a smooth paste. Turn off heat, and whisk paste into the skillet. Whisking constantly, replace the skillet over medium-high heat until the liquid bolls and thickens. If the sauce becomes too thick, dilute with a tittle water or additional wine. Taste and adjust seasoning.

3 Place the duck on a platter, and serve garnished with watercress and fresh grapes; pass the sauce separately. Boiled new potatoes and roast butternut squash are lovely accompaniments.

Makes 3 to 4 servings.

Wild Duck with Lemon and Mint

The bright, complex flavors of this summer dish are perfectly matched with golden roast potatoes and new peas fresh from the garden. If wild duck is unavailable, try to find a source for farm-raised mallards or other wild species.

1 5$\frac{1}{2}$-lb. wild duck, or farm-raised wild species, such as mallard

1 cup freshly squeezed lemon juice (about 5-6 lemons)

$\frac{1}{4}$ cup chopped fresh mint leaves, plus additional sprigs for garnish

8 whole cloves

Salt & freshly ground pepper

2 Tbsp. olive oil

1 If using a domestic duck, see page 19 for technique for rendering the fat. Truss the duck. In a large bowl, combine lemon juice, chopped mint, cloves and salt and pepper to taste. Prick duck skin in several places with a sharp knife, taking care not to puncture the flesh, and place the duck in the bowl, turning to coat well. Marinate for 3 to 4 hours, turning occasionally.

2 Preheat oven to 375°F. Brush the bottom of a roasting pan with the olive oil. Wipe the excess marinade from the duck, and place, breast down on one side, into the roasting pan. Roast for 45 minutes, turning halfway through to the other breast and basting often. At this point, turn duck breast upward, and continue roasting for 30 to 45 minutes, or until the skin is crisp and golden and the bird registers an internal temperature of 160° on an instant-read meat thermometer. Allow duck to rest 20 minutes before carving.

Makes 3 servings.

Grilled Wild Duck à la Percy

Some years ago, my old friend John Percy and I were duck hunting in the marshlands of Ontario. John is a remarkably talented decoy carver and the "artist" of our group; he's also an avid outdoorsman, and when he roughs it, he really roughs it. This trip, we had hiked through miles of deep marsh, in the cold, rainy, windy weather that is perfect for duck hunting. After a time, we did get a couple of beautiful birds, but not before we were chilled to the bone. We built a lean-to with pine boughs and started a fire to dry ourselves off before trekking home. We looked from the birds to the crackling fire and back to the birds again, and before I knew it, John had the ducks crispy and tender, and we had nothing to show for our expedition except full stomachs and happy palates! (This recipe, I have since discovered, works every bit as well on the backyard grill, although the ducks really should be wild or a farm-raised wild species, such as mallards.)

2 4-to-5$\frac{1}{2}$-lb. wild whole ducks, each, or farm-raised
wild species, such as mallards
Salt & freshly ground pepper

If using a domestic duck, refer to page 19 for instructions on how to render the excess fat. Halve the ducks *(see page 23)*, and pat dry. Preheat grill or broiler to high, and rub the grill bars with a lightly oiled cloth to prevent sticking. Season the duck halves well on both sides with salt and pepper, and place skin side down on the hot grill. Close the lid, and grill 5 to 7 minutes, turning once 90 degrees for nice grill marks. Turn birds over, and grill, covered, for another 6 to 7 minutes, or until the juices run pale pink when a breast is pricked with a fork. Duck breast should be enjoyed medium-rare and is a great match for a robust red wine.

Makes 4 servings.

Duck Lahania (Greek Duck with Cabbage)

Lahania is the Greek word for cabbage — a very common accompaniment to duck in the northern part of the country. The region where my wife's family is from is called Thrace and boasts a vast marshland that supports many species, including a majestic wild duck. So desirable is this bird that for generations, the kings of Greece would travel great distances to hunt here! This is a favorite local recipe and is best made with a wild duck. If unavailable, substitute a farm-raised wild species, such as mallard.

1 5$^{1}/_{2}$-lb. large duck, or farm-raised wild species

Salt & freshly ground pepper

$^{1}/_{4}$ cup extra-virgin olive oil

2 medium onions, peeled & sliced thin

1 head Savoy cabbage (tough core discarded), sliced into long, thin shreds

10 whole black peppercorns

1 bay leaf

1 cup George's Tomato Sauce *(see p. 7)*,
or a good-quality purchased sauce

1 If using a domestic duck, refer to page 19 for instructions on rendering the fat. Preheat oven to 375°F. Pat duck dry, truss, and season well with salt and pepper. Place duck on a rack in a roasting pan, and set aside.

2 In a large saucepan, heat olive oil over medium-low heat, and add onions and cabbage. Cook until onions are soft, about 10 minutes. Add peppercorns and bay leaf, and transfer to the roasting pan, around the duck. Pour the tomato sauce over the vegetables, cover the pan with foil, and bake for I hour, basting occasionally. Uncover and continue roasting another 30 to 45 minutes, or until the duck registers an internal temperature of 160° on an instant-read meat thermometer. Allow duck to rest for 20 minutes before serving, surrounded by cabbage and onions and accompanied by lots of mashed potatoes.

Makes 3 to 4 servings.

Grilled Sutton River Duck Breasts

This simple recipe is a favorite of Tim Topornicki, a hunting buddy for many years. The pure, unique flavor of the wild duck is highlighted by the marinade; the smoky grill adds a final perfect touch. Take care not to overcook the breasts — wild duck and farm-raised wild species, such as mallards, should be cooked to about medium-rare, or the flesh will become stringy and tough and the flavor will lessen.

6 large boneless duck breasts, preferably wild, or farm-raised wild species
1 recipe Marinade for Waterfowl *(see p. 4)*
Salt & freshly ground pepper

1 If you are starting with whole ducks, see page 25 for techniques on deboning and removing the breasts. The legs may also be used in this recipe but must be grilled longer. Place breasts in marinade, and refrigerate for 24 hours.

2 Preheat the grill or broiler to high. Remove the duck from the marinade, wipe off the excess, and season well with salt and pepper. Wipe the hot grill bars with a lightly oiled cloth to prevent sticking, and grill the duck breasts, skin side down, for 4 to 5 minutes. Turn once 90 degrees to achieve crisscross markings. Turn breasts over, and grill until breasts are tender but no more than medium-rare, about 4 minutes, depending on thickness. Serve with a fresh green salad and roast new potatoes sprinkled with herbs.

Makes 3 to 4 servings.

Duck Breast Sauté

This is a quick, healthful and delicious dish that can be modified to suit virtually any taste, budget or occasion. Feel free to vary the seasonings and vegetables. A dash of soy sauce and sesame oil, some water chestnuts, baby corn and bok choy make it an Oriental stir-fry; or add fresh corn off the cob, snap peas and other tender garden vegetables for an elegant summer meal.

4 boneless duck breasts

Salt & freshly ground pepper

1 Tbsp. butter

2 Tbsp. olive oil

1 medium onion, thinly sliced

2 large celery stalks, sliced $1/4''$ thick

1 sprig fresh rosemary

1 Tbsp. brandy

1 Remove the skin from the duck breasts by inserting your finger between the skin and flesh and gently pulling it off. The skin can be rendered over very low heat and reserved for sautéing potatoes and adding flavor to soups. Slice the meat in thin strips across the grain, and season with salt and pepper.

2 Heat the butter and oil over medium heat in a wok or nonstick frying pan, and add onions. When the onions are soft, add duck breast pieces, celery and rosemary, and increase heat to medium-high. Sauté, stirring frequently, until duck is cooked rare. Add brandy, and continue sautéing until duck is medium-rare. Serve over rice.

Makes 2 to 5 servings.

Cold Duck Salad

All the elements of this fresh, crisp salad can be prepared ahead of time. All that is needed at serving time is an attractive platter and a glass of chilled white wine. To make this dish work, however, the vegetables must be seasonal and very fresh. Resist the temptation to drown the salad in dressing: a drizzle of good olive oil and a sprinkle of fresh orange juice are all that is necessary.

6 boneless duck breasts

1 recipe Marinade for Waterfowl *(see p. 4)*

Salt & freshly ground pepper

1 Tbsp. butter

2 Tbsp. extra-virgin olive oil, plus additional for drizzling

2 large garden tomatoes, chopped

12 Firm white mushrooms, quartered

1 Spanish onion, peeled & thinly sliced

1 large orange (rind & white pith removed), separated into segments

$^1/_4$ cup chopped fresh coriander or parsley

Juice of 1 orange

1 Remove the skin from the breasts by gently pulling it away from the flesh with your fingers. Place the breasts in marinade, and refrigerate overnight.

2 Remove breasts from marinade, wipe off any excess, and season with salt and pepper. Heat butter and oil in a sauté pan over medium-high heat, and sauté duck breasts until they are medium-rare, about 4 minutes each side. Remove from heat, and allow to cool completely. At this point, breasts may be refrigerated for up to 24 hours.

3 In a large glass bowl or on a decorative platter, combine tomatoes, mushrooms, onions, orange segments and coriander or parsley. Slice the cooked duck breasts into long strips, and arrange on top of the salad. Drizzle with extra-virgin olive oil, sprinkle with freshly squeezed orange juice, and season with salt and pepper.

Makes 4 servings.

Pan-Fried Duck Breasts with Sour Cherries

The tangy sour cherries beautifully offset the richness of the tender duck flesh. If fresh sour cherries are unavailable, use fresh sweet cherries and add a squeeze of lemon juice. Serve with mounds of buttery mashed potatoes to absorb the glorious sauce.

6 boneless duck breasts

2 cups all-purpose flour

Salt & freshly ground pepper

2 Tbsp. olive oil

2 Tbsp. butter

$^1/_4$ cup port

$2^1/_2$ cups fresh pitted sour cherries

$^1/_4$ cup sugar, or to taste

2 Tbsp. brandy

1 Remove the skin from the duck breasts by gently pulling it away from the flesh, taking care not to tear the meat. Combine flour and salt and pepper to taste in a strong plastic bag, and add the duck breasts, a few at a time, tossing to coat thoroughly. Shake off excess. Heat oil and 1 tablespoon of the butter in a sauté pan over medium-high heat, and sauté duck breasts until they are medium-rare and a reddish brown crust forms on each side. Set aside and keep warm.

2 Deglaze the skillet with the port, scraping up brown bits from the bottom. In a small saucepan, combine the contents of the skillet, cherries, sugar and brandy. Bring to a boll, reduce heat, and simmer until cherries begin to split and liquid is reduced to the consistency of a thin sauce. Taste and adjust seasoning with salt, pepper and additional sugar, if necessary. Arrange the duck breasts on a platter, and pour some of the warm cherry sauce over top, passing the remaining sauce separately. Serve immediately.

Makes 4 servings.

Duck and Winter Vegetable Soup with Rice

Wild duck makes a heavenly rich broth, and when the wind is howling outside, nothing is more satisfying then a bowl of this homemade soup.

1 2-lb. wild duck, or a farm-raised wild species, such as mallard

1 large carrot, coarsely chopped

2 medium cooking onions, peeled & thinly sliced

2 large celery stalks, coarsely chopped

1 head cauliflower

1 cup long-grain rice, rinsed

Salt & freshly ground pepper

1 Wash the duck well, and cut into 8 or 9 pieces. Place in a deep pot or Dutch oven with the carrot, onions and celery. Remove the thick stems of the cauliflower, leaving only the tender flowers. Break these into bite-sized pieces, and add to the pot. Add just enough water to cover the duck.

2 Bring to a boll, reduce heat, and simmer for 1 hour. Add rice, and continue cooking until the rice is tender and the meat falls from the bones, about 30 minutes. Season to taste with salt and pepper.

Makes 4 to 6 servings.

Magnotta selection: 1995 Merlot Limited Edition

Roast Wild Goose

Roasting is the classic way to enjoy goose. The first time I ever had roast wild goose was at a cottage at Long Point, a wildlife and waterfowl paradise near the southernmost tip of Ontario. I was on a hunting trip with good friends, and none of us could get over their unique, full flavor. The richly flavored, delicate flesh of wild goose is dramatically different from that of its domestic cousins. If at all possible, prepare this with a wild species. If a domestic goose is the only option, refer to page 19 for instructions on how to render the excess fat. *(See photo page 13.)*

1 5-to-6-lb. wild goose (6-8 lbs. if domestic)

$^{1}/_{4}$ cup butter, melted (only with a wild goose)

$^{1}/_{4}$ cup olive oil (only with a wild goose)

1 large onion, quartered

Salt &, freshly ground pepper

$^{1}/_{2}$ cup water

1 Preheat oven to 375°F. Truss the goose *(see page 20)*. If using a wild goose, rub the skin with melted butter and oil. If using a domestic goose, steam as per the instructions on page 19 for 30 minutes. Place onions inside the cavity, season well with salt and pepper, and place on a rack in a roasting pan. Add the water, cover, and bake for 40 minutes (30 minutes for domestic goose), basting frequently. Uncover and cook an additional 1 to 1$^{1}/_{2}$ hours, or until the goose registers an internal temperature of 165° to 170° on an instant-read meat thermometer, or until the flesh of the breast of a wild goose is tender and pink. With a domestic goose, the juices of a pierced breast will run pale yellow.

2 Allow goose to rest 10 minutes before transferring to a warm platter. Serve with roast potatoes, glazed carrots and steamed green beans.

Makes 6 servings.

Magnotta selection: 1997 Chardonnay Limited Edition

Variation: *Roast Goose With Wild Rice Stuffing*
If using a domestic goose, steam to render fat *(see page 19)*, then proceed with stuffing. In a small saucepan, combine 1 $1/2$ cups water with $1/2$ cup wild rice. Bring to a boll, and simmer until rice just begins to split. Add $1/4$ cup rinsed long-grain rice, and continue cooking until both rices are tender but stilt chewy. Toss with 2 tablespoons butter or rendered goose fat, and allow to cool before spooning into the cavity of the goose. Take care not to overstuff the bird, or it may split during roasting. Truss the goose, season well with salt and pepper, and rub with butter and oil if it is a wild bird. Proceed with above method, but extend cooking time by 30 to 45 minutes.

Rabbit & Hare

Rabbit and hare are two of the most universally popular small game animals. Throughout history, they have proven not only delicious but abundant and versatile. Today, while wild rabbit and hare are not available here commercially, rabbit is being raised all over the continent for wholesale and retail markets. Its surge in esteem in North American cuisine, after generations of having been much less favored here than in Europe, is thanks in part to its nutritive value: rabbit is very lean and low in both calories and cholesterol. It is also a good source of protein, iron and niacin.

North America boasts several species of wild rabbit, such as the native cottontail, and a species imported in the 19th century by European settlers. Wild rabbits can weigh between 5 and 7 pounds at maturity. Their rich, gamey dark meat is much stronger in flavor than that of their domestic cousins. Domestic rabbits are bred for their mild, delicate, slightly chewy flesh, which is fine-textured and almost completely white. They weigh between 3 and 6 pounds.

Hare has always been extremely popular in the European countryside, but in North America, it is available only to the hunter. North American hares, like rabbits, can be native species, such as the varying hare, or may be the larger European-introduced species, which were originally bred for food but are now wild and mostly ignored on this continent. Hares are much larger than rabbits, often weighing between 12 and 15 pounds. They have a strong, gamey flavor and rich, dark purple flesh that lends itself well to long stewing and braising.

Wild rabbit and hare must be hung and marinated before cooking, but the softer, more tender flesh of the domestic breeds does not require this tenderizing. All rabbits are extremely lean, however, and their flesh can become stringy and tough if not prepared with enough moisture. This moisture may be in the form of liquid, as In the common practice of stewing or braising these animals; or it may be present as a small amount of fat added to the dish, such as a cream sauce.

The recipes that follow are some of my favorites for these delicious, versatile creatures. Most dishes using rabbit or hare call for the animal to be disjointed. The butcher can do this for you, or follow the simple instructions on page 78.

Previous page: Saddle of Hare, see recipe page 88

Facing page: Honey Rabbit, see recipe page 80

Disjointing a Rabbit

Rabbits may be disjointed for use in stews or casseroles or so that different parts of the animal can be used in different preparations. A thin-bladed, sharp boning knife makes the task easy and safe.

1. Lay the rabbit breast down on a cutting board, with the hind legs pointing away from you.

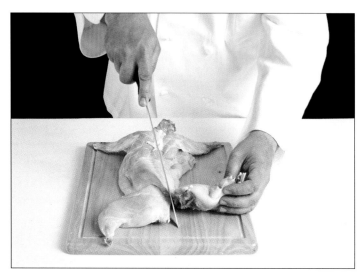

2. To remove the legs, make your first cut at the top of the thigh and gently work your knife toward you, separating the leg at the joint. Repeat on the other side.

3. Turn the rabbit 180 degrees so that the arms are pointing away from you. Hold one arm up, and work your knife around the joint, never pushing hard but letting the weight of the rabbit's body provide tension for the knife. Repeat with the other arm.

4. Cut between the breast section and the back, or saddle, section. The breast may be separated by carefully cutting down the backbone from the underside of the rabbit. While the breast has little or no usable meat on it, it is useful in preparing stocks and sauces.

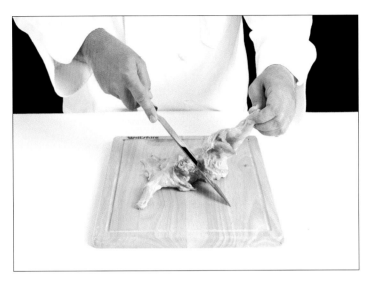 

5. To remove the two loins from the saddle section, use a small, sharp knife to pry the long, round cylinders of meat from their place just alongside the backbone. Like the breast, the backbone is good for flavoring stocks or sauces. The boneless loins may be cut into four pieces for certain dishes where quick cooking is desired, such as sautéing.

6. The rabbit cut into 10 pieces: The six serving pieces are two legs, the two arms and the saddle, or two loins; breasts, backbone and collarbone may be used for stocks, soups and sauces.

Honey Rabbit

My wife and I once had the pleasure of dining in an elegant Moroccan restaurant designed as a true sultan's tent. It was spectacular, but the belly dancers, the candlelight and the rich tapestries all paled in comparison to the meal-succulent rabbit with honey. I urge you to enjoy this unusual dish as it would be eaten in Morocco: seated on cushions scattered on the floor, with the candles flickering. *See photo page 77.*

16 pearl onions

1 rabbit, disjointed *(see p. 78)*

Salt & freshly ground pepper

2 Tbsp. butter

2 Tbsp. olive oil

2 cloves garlic, peeled

2 shallots, peeled & finely chopped

$^1/_2$ cup chicken stock, preferably homemade, or canned low-salt broth

$^1/_2$ cup strong-flavored honey

8 plump, Moist prunes

1 Bring a small pot of water to a boll. Add pearl onions, and boil 2 minutes. Drain and plunge into a bowl of ice water to stop the cooking, then slip off the skins. Set aside.

2 Wash the rabbit pieces, pat dry, and season with salt and pepper. In a large skillet, heat butter and olive oil over medium-high heat, and add the rabbit. Brown on all sides, then remove from the skillet. Reduce heat to medium, and add the pearl onions and garlic cloves. Sauté until outer skins of the onions are golden brown, then remove. Cook the garlic until beginning to soften, then add chopped shallots, and stir to brown. Pour the stock into the skillet, and

deglaze, scraping up any brown bits from the bottom. Return the rabbit and pearl onions to the skillet, add honey and prunes, and simmer, partially covered, for 20 to 30 minutes, or until rabbit is tender. If sauce is too thin, increase heat and reduce slightly before pouring over rabbit. Serve immediately in a shallow dish, with steamed couscous or rice.

Makes 4 servings.

Magnotta selection: 1998 Riesling Medium Dry Limited Edition

Stifado of Rabbit

Stifado, meaning "hunter-style with onions," is a heady Greek stew often made with beef or lamb. I have adapted it for rabbit, and the result is splendid: the exotic combination of cinnamon, wine, rich tomato and delicate rabbit is heavenly. Unfortunately, unless you know a hunter, you will be using a domestic rabbit; buy the largest one you can find.

1 large rabbit, disjointed *(see p. 78)*

1 recipe Marinade for Small Game *(see p. 5)*

16 pearl onions

Salt & freshly ground pepper

2 Tbsp. butter

1 Tbsp. olive oil

1 cup dry red wine

1 cup George's Tomato Sauce *(see p. 7)*, or a good-quality purchased sauce

1 large cinnamon stick

12 whole peppercorns

1 cup water

1 Marinate rabbit 3 to 4 hours or overnight.

2 Bring a small pot of water to a boil, add pearl 60 onions, and blanch 45 seconds to 1 minute. Remove onions, and plunge into a bowl of ice water to stop the cooking. Slip the skins off, and set the onions aside.

3 Remove the rabbit from the marinade, wipe off excess, and season with salt and pepper. In a large skillet, heat butter and oil together over medium-high heat. Add the rabbit pieces, and brown on all sides, then place in a deep casserole. Pour the wine into the skillet, and deglaze, scraping up any brown bits from the bottom. Pour the contents of the skillet into the casserole, and add tomato sauce, onions, cinnamon and peppercorns. Add 1 cup water, cover, and bring to a boil. Reduce heat, and simmer, partially covered, for $2^1/_2$ hours, or until the rabbit is meltingly tender. Serve with roast potatoes or steamed rice.

Makes 4 servings.

Normandy Rabbit with Red Wine

This classic recipe brings back vivid memories of the French countryside and the French drinking wine. I traveled to the Normandy region in France mainly intending to visit the graves of the Canadian soldiers who gave their lives in World War II. My secondary, and more lighthearted, aim was to sample the world-famous local cuisine. I was not disappointed. A lunch at a small bistro offered the opportunity to experience the Norman preference for rabbit-and another wonderful recipe to take home.

16 pearl onions

2 cups + 1 Tbsp. all-purpose flour

Salt & freshly ground pepper

1 4-to-5-lb. rabbit, disjointed *(see p. 78)*

114 cup butter

2 Tbsp. chopped chives

$1^1/_4$ cups dry red wine

$^1/_2$ cup water

1 Bring a small pot of water to a boil, add pearl onions, and blanch for 45 seconds to 1 minute. Drain and plunge onions into a bowl of ice water to stop the cooking. Slip the skins off, and reserve.

2 Preheat oven to 350°F. Place 2 cups of flour into a strong plastic bag, and season with salt and pepper. Add the rabbit pieces, a few at a time, and shake to coat them well. Shake off excess. In a large skillet, heat 3 tablespoons of the butter over medium-high heat. When the foam subsides, add the rabbit pieces and brown on all sides. Transfer rabbit to a

casserole, and add the pearl onions and chives. Pour off all but 2 tablespoons of the juices from the skillet, and add 1 tablespoon flour. Cook over low heat, stirring constantly, until flour is browned. Whisk in the red wine and $^1/_2$ cup of water, bring to a boil, and deglaze the skillet. Pour this mixture into the casserole over the rabbit, and cover. Bake for $1^1/_2$ to $1^3/_4$ hours, or until rabbit is tender. Serve immediately with potatoes, a green salad and some good crusty bread for mopping up the delicious sauce.

Makes 4 servings.

Magnotta selection: 1998 Cabernet Sauvignon Special Reserve

Braised Rabbit with Lemon

In this lovely dish, the delicate flavor of the rabbit is heightened by the equally delicate fresh lemon. The result is a perfect summer dinner when paired with new potatoes in their jackets and steamed green beans.

1 4-to-5-lb. rabbit

1 recipe Marinade for Small Game *(see p. 5)*

Salt & freshly ground pepper

2 Tbsp. olive oil

3 Tbsp. butter

2 medium onions, finely chopped

$\frac{1}{2}$ cup dry white wine

Juice of 3 lemons

1 tsp. Finely chopped oregano

1 Marinate rabbit for 3 to 4 hours or overnight.

2 Preheat oven to 375°F. Remove pieces from marinade wipe off excess, and season with salt and pepper. In a large skillet, heat oil and 2 tablespoons of the butter over medium-high heat. Add rabbit pieces, and sauté until evenly browned. Transfer rabbit to a shallow baking dish.

3 Drain off the excess fat from the skillet, then sauté onions over medium-low beat until they are soft and beginning to brown. Add to the rabbit pieces in the baking dish. Pour white wine into the skillet, increase heat, and deglaze, scraping up any brown bits from the bottom. Pour into the baking dish. Add lemon juice, oregano and remaining tablespoon butter, and cover the dish with foil. Bake for 1 hour, uncover, and turn rabbit pieces around in the liquid. Continue cooking, uncovered, another 30 minutes, or until rabbit is very tender. Serve immediately,

Makes 4 servings.

Rabbit with Sherry

This is a simple, classic recipe that treats rabbit much the same way as it has been prepared in the Xeres (now Jerez) country of Spain for generations. Green beans with almonds make a perfect accompaniment.

1 4-to-5-lb. rabbit, disjointed *(see p. 78)*

1 recipe Marinade for Small Game *(see p. 5)*

Salt & freshly ground pepper

3 Tbsp. olive oil

2 Tbsp. butter

$^1/_3$ cup sherry

1 medium onion, peeled & thinly sliced

1-2 cloves garlic, peeled & finely chopped

10 whole peppercorns

1 Marinate rabbit 3 to 4 hours or overnight in the Marinade for Small Game.

2 Preheat oven to 375°F. Remove pieces from the marinade, wipe off excess, and season with salt and pepper. Heat the oil and butter in a skillet over medium-high heat. Add the rabbit pieces, and sauté until evenly browned, then transfer to a shallow baking dish. Pour sherry into the skillet, and deglaze, scraping up any brown bits from the bottom. Add contents of the skillet to the baking dish, along with onions, garlic and peppercorns. Cover the dish with foil, and bake for 1 hour. Uncover, stir the rabbit in the liquid, reduce temperature to 325°, and continue cooking for another 30 minutes, or until rabbit is very tender. Taste and adjust seasoning with salt and pepper.

Makes 4 servings.

Rabbit España

This delicious stew is filled with the warm, strong flavors of Spain and the Mediterranean — creamy eggplant, piquant olives and rich tomato. Use the largest rabbit you can find, and consider yourself lucky if you can get a wild rabbit!

1 large rabbit

Salt & freshly ground pepper

2 Tbsp. butter

$1/_4$ cup olive oil

3 medium Spanish onions, peeled & thinly sliced

2 cloves garlic, minced

1 medium eggplant, chopped into 1″ pieces

1 cup dry red wine

$1/_2$ cup tomato paste

$1/_2$ cup pitted black olives

1 Tbsp. chopped fresh oregano

1 Preheat oven to 375°F. Pat rabbit pieces dry, and season with salt and pepper. In a large Dutch oven, heat butter and 1 tablespoon of the oil, and add onions. Cook over medium-low heat until soft; add garlic, and cook 2 minutes, taking care not burn it. Remove onions and garlic, and set aside.

2 Add the remaining oil to the skillet, and add eggplant pieces. Sauté over medium-high heat until tender and beginning to brown, then set aside with the onions and garlic. Increase heat, and deglaze the pot with the wine, scraping the bottom to remove any brown bits, Reduce heat, and add whole rabbit, reserved sautéed vegetables, tomato paste, olives and oregano. Cover with foil, and place on the middle rack of the oven for 45 minutes. Remove the cover, and add $1/_2$ cup water if stew appears too thick or dry. Reduce temperature, and bake another 30 to 45 minutes, or until rabbit is very tender. Serve with mashed potatoes.

Makes 4 servings.

Hasenpfeffer

For this rich and highly flavored German dish, translated literally as "hare pepper," a hare makes a crucial difference. If a hare is simply unavailable, substitute two of the largest rabbits you can find. The sour cream, however, is not optional — its richness balances the dish perfectly

1 12-to-14-lb. hare, or 2 large rabbits, about 5 lbs. each, disjointed *(see p. 78)*

2 recipes Marinade for Small Game *(see p. 5)*

2 cups all-purpose flour

Salt & freshly ground pepper

2 oz. salt pork, cut into 1≤ cubes, or 4 slices bacon

1 large onion, finely chopped

$^1/_2$ lb. firm white mushrooms, quartered

2 Tbsp. butter

$^3/_4$ cup sour cream

1 Marinate hare overnight, or for up to 2 days.

2 Remove hare from marinade, wiping off excess and reserving half of the marinade. Combine flour and salt and pepper in a strong plastic bag; add hare pieces, and toss to coat thoroughly. Shake off excess flour. In a large casserole or Dutch oven, sauté the salt pork or bacon over medium heat until golden brown. Remove the pieces with a slotted spoon, and add onions to the fat. Sauté over medium-low heat until onions are soft and beginning to color; remove and reserve. Add the mushrooms to the casserole, and cook over medium-high heat until golden; remove and set aside.

3 Drain off excess fat from the casserole, and add butter. Add the hare pieces, and sauté over medium-high heat until well browned. Pour in the reserved marinade, deglazing by scraping up any brown bits from the bottom. Return the salt pork or bacon, the onions and the mushrooms to the casserole, and bring to a boll. Reduce heat, cover, and simmer until the hare is tender, about 1 to $1^1/_2$ hours. Taste and adjust seasoning.

4 Transfer hare to a warmed platter. Whisk the sour cream into the liquid in the casserole, and cook over low heat until well blended. Return hare to sauce, and serve immediately with buttered noodles or spaetzle.

Makes 6 to 8 servings.

Saddle of Hare

When I was a young lad growing up in the country in southern Ontario my uncles and brother-in-law hunted rabbit and hare on a regular basis. I was still a novice hunter, but I was becoming as interested in the cooking of wild game as in the hunting of it. There was always a freezer full of wonderful wild rabbit to experiment with, and this recipe became a unanimous favorite. The saddle, or loin, is the most tender part of the rabbit; if you cannot get the saddle of a wild hare, use two loins of domestic rabbit. *(See photo page 75.)*

2-3 leeks, roots trimmed & dark green ends discarded

2 cups all-purpose flour

Salt & freshly ground pepper

1 saddle of wild hare, or 2 saddles of domestic rabbit

3 Tbsp. olive oil

1 cup dry red wine

1 cup chicken stock, preferably homemade, or canned low-salt broth

1 large onion, quartered

3 cloves garlic

$^1/_4$ cup butter

2 tsp. cornstarch

1 To clean leeks, slice in half vertically, then slice into thin half circles. Float the chopped leeks in a large bowl of cool water, and swirl them around your hand. The dirt will settle on the bottom; carefully lift the leeks out before draining the water out. Dry thoroughly on paper towels before proceeding.

2 Preheat the oven to 350°F. Combine flour and salt and pepper in a strong plastic bag, and add the rabbit loin, shaking to coat well. Shake off excess flour. Heat olive oil in a skillet, and brown loin on all sides. Transfer to a shallow baking dish. Add the wine to the skillet and deglaze, scraping up any brown bits from the bottom. Pour into the baking dish, along with the stock, onions and garlic cloves. Cover and bake for $1^1/_2$ hours, or until the rabbit is tender.

3 Meanwhile, melt butter in a heavy-bottomed saucepan. Add the chopped leeks, and sauté over medium heat until beginning to brown, then add a few tablespoons of water. Reduce heat, cover, and simmer until leeks are meltingly soft. Keep warm.

4 Transfer the saddle of hare to a serving platter, and keep warm. Combine cornstarch with a small amount of cool water to make a smooth paste. Whisking constantly, pour this into the liquid in the baking dish and slowly bring to a boil. Continue whisking until sauce is of coating consistency. Taste and adjust seasoning with salt and pepper. To serve, pour some of the sauce over the saddle of hare, sur- round with the leeks and pass the remaining sauce separately.

Makes 2 to 3 servings.

Magnotta selection: 1999 Meritage VQA (a blend of Cabernet Sauvignon, Cabernet Franc and Merlot)

Big Game

For as many years as human beings have hunted, foraged and lived together, a successful hunt was cause for feasting and thanks. While we modern North Americans need only forage as far as the supermarket for our meat, a feast of bison, boar or deer can still elicit in us a sense of anticipation and respect. Today, big game meats are being increasingly sought after, and thanks to ranchers in North America and around the world, they are becoming more and more available. Their popularity is understandable. They are highly nutritious: low in cholesterol, fat and calories and high in protein and nutrients. Most big game is raised organically, with a minimum of human or chemical intervention. At a time when beef is being showered with criticism from all sides, meats such as venison and bison are ideal substitutes. Their unique, rich and complex flavors are quickly making them indispensable to today's foremost chefs looking for more interesting ingredients.

Domestic animals are generally less gamey in flavor and more tender than their wild counterparts. Since the meat of all species of big game becomes tougher and very strong in taste as they age, younger animals are usually preferable.

Venison

In medieval times, a spit-roasted stag was often the centerpiece for grand banquets, the symbol of all that was wild and powerful. Venison is rapidly becoming the chic new trend in contemporary cuisine. Native to North America, Europe and Asia, different species of deer are now being farmed all over the world. New Zealand red deer accounts for about 75 to 80 percent of all deer purchased in North America and is available both farmed and, less frequently, wild. Native and

imported species, such as roebuck, whitetail, fallow, axis and sika, are also being raised. As with any big game, deer's taste and texture will vary with its environment and diet. Grassy, herbal and floral overtones can sometimes be detected in deer that have been raised on pasture and hay. Venison meat is very lean and has a rich flavor that is pronouncedly gamey if wild.

Moose, Caribou, Antelope and Elk

Though moose, caribou, antelope and elk may occasionally share the label "venison," there are subtle differences in the taste and texture of each. (Venison is most properly any species of deer; confirm with your butcher or supplier to make sure you are getting what you requested.) Moose and caribou roam wild all over northern Canada and Alaska. Both have dark, rich meat and are a cross between deer and beef in flavor. Antelope, only available wild, are smaller, delicate animals and are found in more southerly regions of the plains provinces and states. Their deep flavor can be compared to that of goat, and the meat is dense and slightly chewy. Elk meat is delicate, rich and strongly gamey. Like antelope, it is almost never available commercially, but if you ever have the opportunity, I encourage you to try it.

Bison

What we know as buffalo is actually a North American species of bison. Bison have been a part of our human and culinary heritage since prehistory; they have changed little from the majestic beasts depicted in fluid cave paintings from thousands of years ago. At one time, bison literally supported North America's native and settler population, providing food, milk, clothing,

Previous page: Roast Venison Tenderloin, see page 100 for recipe.

shelter, fuel and tools. Overhunting and careless development almost caused the extinction of this noble species. Thanks to a move toward good agricultural practices and to the efforts of a few very committed ranchers, the species not only survived but is now thriving on ranches all over the United States and western Canada. Bison meat is coarse and dark red, with a rich delicate taste almost indistinguishable from beef.

Wild Boar

The very mention of wild boar conjures up images of almost mythical beasts, savage and unfamiliar. In fact, although the boar that still run wild in North America and Europe are quite dangerous, they are also delicious! Several species are available both wild and farm-raised in North America, the most common being a breed of domestic pig that has become wild over the past century. While it is now more popular to raise, boar is still relatively uncommon. Wild boar meat is wonderfully unique: somewhat like pork in taste but closer to veal in texture. Its dark pink meat may have a slightly nutty taste, as acorns and other fallen nuts and seeds are the wild boar's standard diet.

Ostrich

Ostrich is one of the most recent additions to big game ranching in North America, and while these creatures are far from their native lands of Africa, they are thriving. Many upscale restaurants have added ostrich to their menus and have met with great success. Ostrich flesh is dark and rich, with a slightly chewy texture. It actually bears more resemblance to big game meats than to game birds and benefits from many of the same preparations.

Never before in history have so many exciting, healthful and truly delicious species of big game been available to the food enthusiast and home cook. The recipes on the following pages have been collected so that you can explore these wonderful meats and taste their unique flavors simply and purely. Do riot be discouraged if all these animals are not available in your area -with the exception of wild boar and ostrich, they may be interchanged (for a quick reference substitution chart, *see page 10*).

❧ Preparing Big Game ❧

Much of the more complex preparation of big game meats can be done by your butcher or mail-order company. In every case, examine the piece of meat when you get it home to ensure it is properly trimmed. When preparing cuts of big game meat for cooking, use a sharp knife and a large cutting board. On many cuts of big game, a thin, silvery membrane called silver skin covers the meat. Unlike the thicker white connective tissue, this membrane cannot be cooked tender and, if left on the meat, will cause it to buckle during cooking. Meat without the silver skin removed is tough and unpleasant to eat.

Removing Silver Skin

Removing silver skin is simple, and in many cases, the membrane needs only a little cutting to come away. Lay the piece of meat on a cutting board, and slide the blade of a thin, sharp knife between the silver skin and the flesh in one area. Cut to make a flap of silver skin, then work the knife along the membrane to slice it away from the meat in a long, smooth strip. Repeat this process until all the visible silver skin is removed.

Cutting Steaks Against the Grain

The "grain" of a piece of meat is the direction in which the fibers run. When cutting steaks from a larger piece of meat, first ensure all silver skin has been removed. Find the cutting side of the meat (the side where the fibers end), and place this side up to be sliced. Use a long, thin blade to seesaw through the meat in long strokes, cutting the desired thickness of steak. Keep the knife level and straight, and let the sawing motion and the sharpness of the knife do the work- there should be very little downward pressure

Butterflying

Steaks, chops, sections of loin and other thick, boneless cuts of meat may be butterflied to create a thinner cut that will cook more evenly and be easier to eat. To butterfly a thick cut, place the meat on a cutting board and use a thin, sharp knife to cut slightly more than halfway through the width of the steak. Flatten out the steak, with the cut center facing up, and pound the steak gently to spread it out.

Facing page: Moose Steak Flambé, see recipe page 96

Moose Steak Flambé

This is an excellent way to introduce game to the uninitiated. It works beautifully with any big game steaks, such as elk, bison, venison or caribou. The pounding allows a fairly tough cut of meat to be tenderized and cooked quickly. Cut boneless steaks about $1/2''$ thick, and have everything else in the meal ready to serve before cooking the steaks. Homemade French-fried potatoes are the perfect partner to this recipe.

3 boneless strip sirloin moose steaks (or other game steaks), cut $1/2''$ thick

2 Tbsp. olive oil

2 Tbsp. butter

2 Tbsp. brandy

2 scallions (green onions), finely chopped

1 Tbsp. chopped fresh parsley

1 cup beef stock, preferably homemade, or canned low-salt broth

1 tsp. Worcestershire sauce

Salt & freshly ground pepper

1 Pound the steaks to $1/4''$ thickness using a wooden mallet. With a fork, pierce one end of each steak, and roll it into a cylinder.

2 In a large skillet, heat the oil and butter over medium-high heat. Unroll one steak into the hot pan, rolling away from you to avoid splattering.

3 Cook for about 1 minute, flip, and continue cooking about 1 more minute, until steak is browned on both sides. Remove steak to a platter, and repeat process until all steaks are cooked and set aside.

4 Pour off the excess fat from the skillet, add the brandy, and flambé. (Do not be concerned if it does not light.) Reduce heat, and allow the brandy to deglaze the pan. Add the scallions to the pan, and cook for 2 minutes, then add the parsley, and return the steaks to the pan.

5 Pour the beef stock over the steaks, and bring to a boil.

6 Reduce quickly by a third to a half, and stir in Worcestershire sauce. Season to taste with salt and pepper. Transfer steaks to a warm platter, and pour pan juices over them.

Magnotta selection: 1996 Magnotta Millennium (Cabernet Sauvignon)

Makes 4 to 6 servings.

Peppered Caribou Steaks

The seemingly strange marriage of flavors — a combination of sweet, spicy and rich — conspires to create a truly wonderful steak. Caribou is readily available by mail order, but this recipe may also be prepared with bison, elk or venison steaks.

$^1/_4$ cup soy sauce

1/4 cup beef stock, preferably homemade, or canned low-salt broth

$^1/_2$ cup port

5 10-to-12-oz. caribou steaks

15 pearl onions

Salt

$^1/_2$ cup freshly crushed peppercorns (the bottom of a heavy pot works well – use a rolling motion to crush)

3 Tbsp. olive oil

3 Tbsp. butter

$^1/_4$ cup mustard powder

$^1/_4$ cup water

1 In a shallow, nonreactive dish, whisk together soy sauce, beef stock and port, and add steaks, turning to coat thoroughly. Refrigerate for 24 hours or overnight, turning occasionally.

2 Bring a small pot of water to a boll, add pearl onions, and simmer for 2 minutes. Drain and plunge the onions into a bowl of ice water to stop the cooking. Carefully slip the papery skins off, leaving as many layers of the onion as possible. Set aside.

3 Remove steaks from the marinade, wiping off excess, and season well with salt. Place the peppercorns in a shallow dish, and press the steaks into them, coating each side. In a heavy, preferably cast-iron frying pan, heat the olive oil over medium-high to high heat. Cook the steaks to the desired doneness, and remove to a warm platter.

4 Meanwhile, melt half the butter in a small saucepan over medium-low heat, add the pearl onions, and sauté until golden.

5 In another small saucepan, whisk together mustard powder and water. Add the remaining butter, and slowly bring to a simmer. Reduce heat, and whisk until the mixture is smooth.

6 Pour the mustard sauce over steaks, and surround with caramelized onions.

Makes 5 large servings.

Magnotta selection: 1995 Cabernet Merlot Limited Edition

Roast Venison Tenderloin

Late fall, when the cornfields become bare and the first frosts begin, is the perfect time to invite friends over to enjoy the season's bounty. This intensely flavorful roast is a spectacular way to celebrate the occasion! *(See photo page 91.)*

1 recipe Marinade for Big Game *(see p. 5)*, substituting the lemon juice and tarragon
with 1 medium onion, peeled & thinly sliced, and $^1/_2$ cup port

1 3-to-4-lb. boneless venison tenderloin, all silver skin removed *(see p. 94)*

Salt & freshly ground pepper

4 thin strips salt pork, or 6 strips bacon

2 lbs. small new potatoes, peeled if desired

1 lb. fresh Brussels sprouts

$^1/_4$ cup butter

1 cup beef stock, preferably homemade, or canned low-salt broth

1 tsp. cornstarch

Paprika for garnish

1 Combine the elements of the marinade in a shallow dish, add venison tenderloin, and turn to coat. Marinate 24 hours or overnight, turning occasionally.

2 Preheat oven to 400°F. Remove venison from the marinade, pat dry, and reserve the liquid. Season the tenderloin well with salt and pepper, and lay the salt pork or bacon over the meat, overlapping the strips. Tie the tenderloin to hold the barding in place, tucking the thinnest end of the tenderloin under to make a fairly even cylinder. Place on a rack, and roast for 25 minutes, then reduce oven temperature to 375°. Continue roasting for another 20 to 30

minutes, or until an instant-read meat thermometer inserted in the thickest part of the roast reads 125°. Transfer venison to a platter, cover with foil, and let rest for 15 to 20 minutes.

3 Meanwhile, bring two pots of salted water to a boil; add potatoes to one and Brussels sprouts to the other. Cook both until they are tender; drain and toss each with 2 tablespoons butter. Keep warm.

4 Pour off the excess fat from the roasting pan, and add the reserved marinade. Deglaze by bringing to a boil and scraping up any brown bits from the bottom. Pour into a small saucepan, and boil until the liquid is reduced by half. Add the stock, and reduce again by a quarter. In a small bowl, combine cornstarch and a little water to make a smooth paste. Remove sauce from heat, whisk cornstarch mixture into the sauce, then replace over the heat, and bring to a gentle boil, whisking until the sauce thickens.

5 To serve, surround the roast with the potatoes and Brussels sprouts, dusting the potatoes with paprika if they have been peeled, and pass the sauce in a sauceboat.

Makes 6 to 8 servings.

Magnotta selection: 1998 II Cacciatore (a blend of Cabernet Sauvignon, Merlot and Carmenère)

Venison Casserole

In southern Ontario, the hunt is always the first week of November, and for me, this dish is linked in memory with many fall nights spent in the small-town kitchens of close friends. Caribou, moose or even elk may be substituted for the venison.

2$^1/_2$ cups dry red wine

15 whole peppercorns

1 medium onion, peeled & finely chopped

1 stalk celery, chopped

1 3-lb. boneless venison shoulder, all silver skin removed *(see p. 94)*

Salt & freshly ground pepper

4 slices salt pork, or 5 slices bacon

18 pearl onions

3 Tbsp. butter

1 lb. firm white mushrooms, sliced

1 cup George's Tomato Sauce *(see p. 7)*, or a good-quality purchased sauce

1/2 cup beef stock, preferably homemade, or canned low-salt broth

2 tsp. cornstarch

1 Tbsp. brandy

1 In a shallow, nonreactive dish, combine red wine (reserving 1 tablespoon for later), peppercorns, chopped onions and celery. Place venison in this marinade, turning to coat thoroughly. Marinate 24 hours or overnight, turning occasionally.

2 Preheat oven to 350°F. Remove venison from marinade, strain, and reserve liquid. Pat the venison dry, season with salt and pepper, and lay the salt pork or bacon over top. Tie securely to make a uniform roast. Place on a rack in a roasting pan, and roast for 1 to 11/2 hours, or until an instant-read meat thermometer inserted in the thickest part of the shoulder reads 125°. Baste occasionally with 1 cup of the reserved marinade. Remove roast to a carving board, and cover with foil. Allow roast to rest for 15 minutes before cutting into 1$^1/_2$″ cubes.

Magnotta selection: 1998 II Cacciatore (a blend of Cabernet Sauvignon, Merlot and Carmenère)

3 Meanwhile, bring a small pot of water to a boll, add pearl onions, and simmer for 2 to 2$^1/_2$ minutes. Drain and plunge into a bowl of ice water to stop the cooking. Carefully slip the skins off, leaving as many layers of onion as possible. Reserve.

4 In a large skillet, melt butter over medium heat, and add mushrooms. Sauté until all the liquid has evaporated and the mushrooms are beginning to become golden. Reserve.

5 Pour the excess fat from the roasting pan, and place the pan juices into a large saucepan, along with the tomato sauce, reserved marinade liquid and beef stock. Bring to a boil, and reduce by a third. In a small bowl, combine cornstarch with a little water to make a smooth paste, and whisk this paste into the saucepan off the heat. Bring to a boll and whisk constantly until the sauce thickens. Reduce heat, and add the reserved pearl onions, mushrooms, venison cubes, brandy and reserved tablespoon red wine, and heat through. Taste and adjust seasoning with salt and pepper, and serve immediately with mashed potatoes or buttered noodles.

Makes 6 to 8 servings.

Venison Stew à la George

This dish is named after me for one simple reason: It is my favorite! Venison is a dark, wonderfully rich meat that deserves a place of honor. This hearty stew has no intense seasonings, no wine or strong spices to mask the taste of the meat. It is a true celebration of wild game.

2-3 lbs. boneless venison meat (shoulder & loin both work well), all silver skin removed *(see p. 94)*

1 recipe Marinade for Big Game *(see p. 5)*

Salt & freshly ground pepper

2 Tbsp. butter

3 Tbsp. olive oil

$^1/_2$ cup water

4 medium onions, peeled & chopped in 1″ pieces

8 large, firm white mushrooms, sliced

6 medium potatoes, peeled & cut into 1″ cubes

2 large carrots, peeled & sliced $^1/_2$″ thick

2 large outer celery stalks, sliced $^1/_2$″ thick

1 bay leaf

10 whole peppercorn

1 Cut the venison in 2″ cubes, and place in a shallow, nonreactive dish. Add the marinade, stirring to coat the meat, and refrigerate for 24 hours or overnight.

2 Drain the venison, allowing the excess marinade to drip off. Season cubes with salt and pepper. In a large skillet, heat butter and oil over medium-high heat, and sauté the venison until well browned. Transfer to a deep casserole or Dutch oven.

3 Pour off the excess fat from the skillet, and deglaze skillet with $^1/_2$ cup water, scraping up any brown bits from the bottom of the pan. Add b the casserole with the venison, along with the onions, mushrooms, potatoes, carrots, celery, bay leaf and peppercorns. Add enough water to barely cover the contents, and bring to a boil. Reduce heat, and simmer, partially covered, for $1^1/_2$ to 2 hours, until the venison is very tender. Taste and adjust seasoning with salt and pepper.

Makes 6 to 8 servings.

Lentil Soup with Venison Stock

This thick, hearty soup fairly cries out for a snowy night, a loaf or two of good, crusty bread and a tableful of hungry friends!

3 cups homemade venison stock *(see below)*

1 cup brown or green lentils

Tbsp. olive oil

1 large onion, peeled & finely chopped

1 cup water

2 bay leaves

$1/2$ cup George's Tomato Sauce *(see p. 7)*, or a good-quality purchased sauce

2 cloves garlic, finely chopped

Salt & freshly ground pepper

For garnish:

Extra-virgin olive oil for drizzling

3 green onions (roots & any limp tips discarded), finely chopped

Kalamata olives

1 To prepare venison stock: Ask your butcher or game meat supplier for venison bones. Place bones on a baking sheet, and roast in a preheated 375°F oven until well browned. Transfer bones to a deep stockpot, and deglaze the baking sheet with water, scraping up all of the caramelized bits from the bottom. Pour into the stockpot, and add enough water to barely cover the bones. Bring to a boil, then reduce to a gentle simmer, and simmer for 4 to 8 hours. Strain the stock, discard the bones, and refrigerate for several hours or overnight. The fat will congeal on the top of the stock and can be easily skimmed off before using.

2 Rinse lentils well in cold, running water, picking through them carefully to remove any stones. In a medium saucepan, heat olive oil over medium-low heat, and sweat onions until soft and beginning to color. Add the stock, water, lentils, bay leaves, tomato sauce and garlic, and bring to a boil. Reduce heat, and simmer for 1 to $1^1/2$ hours, or until lentils are very tender, adding more water if the soup is looking too thick. Taste and adjust seasoning with salt and pepper. Serve in shallow soup bowls, drizzled with extra-virgin olive oil and garnished with green onions and Kalamata olives.

Makes 4 servings.

Magnotta selection: 1999 Merlot VQA

Rack of Venison à la Perdicaris

It is in the Biggar, Saskatchewan, restaurant of my dear friend Demetre Perdicaris that I have eaten some of the best game meals of my life. Demetre is a huge-hearted bear of a man whose innate respect for game animals is matched only by his understanding of their culinary possibilities. For this recipe, he combines the Greek technique of inserting slivers of garlic into the meat with the native North American custom of baking wrapped foods buried in charcoal pits. The result is divine.

1 3-to-4-lb. rack of venison

$^1/_4$ cup chilled butter

4 cloves garlic, peeled & cut into slivers

$^1/_4$ cup olive oil

Salt & freshly ground pepper

$^1/_4$ cup dry red wine

3 or 4 large sheets of extra-strong aluminum foil

1 Have your butcher or mail-order supplier clean, or "French," the rack for you. In a charcoal pit, or kettle barbecue, prepare a fairly deep bed of coals; light and allow to get hot. Lay the foil pieces, slightly overlapping, in the shape of a large rectangle. Fold edges together to create a good seat. Smear foil with butter, leaving a thick film.

2 With the blade of a small, sharp knife, stab the rack all over, and insert the garlic slivers into the slits. Try to make the slits as evenly spaced as possible. Don't worry about the slivers being too big — the roasting will make the garlic mild and mellow. Rub the olive oil into the meat, and season well with salt and pepper. Place the rack in the center of the foil sheet, and pour the wine carefully over the meat.

Fold the edges of the foil up over the rack, and fold the ends together to make a tight seat. If necessary, reinforce the packet with more foil to ensure that it is leakproof.

3 With a small shovel or poker, spread the coals apart, and bury the wrapped rack of venison among the coals. Cook for 1 to $1^1/_2$ hours, depending on desired doneness (1 hour will usually produce a medium-rare rack). Serve with baked or mashed potatoes.

Makes 6 to 8 servings.

Venison "Scaloppine" à la Angelo

Angelo was a cook whose restaurant, The Spaghetti House, I worked in while I was getting my degree. He was a character out of a movie: a heavy-smoking, hard-drinking Greek who had no business cooking at all, let alone Italian food. I'm not sure if he knew the dish he called scaloppine was actually something else altogether, but one night, when I brought him some venison meat, we decided we'd create Venison Scaloppine. Much to my surprise, the result was a wonderful discovery.

1 lb. venison tenderloin, trimmed of all silver skin *(see p. 94)*

$1/_4$ cup olive oil

1 medium onion, peeled & coarsely chopped

1 cup coarsely chopped green pepper

1 cup quartered firm white mushrooms

$1/_3$ cup dry white wine

Salt & freshly ground pepper

Cut the venison into 1″ cubes. In a large skillet, heat 1 tablespoons of the olive oil over medium heat, and add onions. When they begin to soften, add peppers and mushrooms, and sauté until peppers are soft and the liquid from the mushrooms has evaporated. Remove and set aside. Add the remaining 2 tablespoons olive oil to the skillet, and increase heat to medium-high. Sauté the venison cubes until well browned on all sides. Add wine, and reduce slightly, scraping up any brown bits from the bottom of the skillet. Return the vegetables to the skillet, partially cover, and simmer 2 minutes. Taste and adjust seasoning with salt and pepper. Serve with buttered noodles or rice.

Makes 4 servings.

Theodore's Big Game Sausages with Leeks

Sausages made with fresh leeks are typical fare of the region in Greece where my wife's family originates. Her father, Theodore, and I used to make these together, following a wonderful family recipe. I have included it in this book as a tribute to him. The sausages may also be made using any other big game meat in place of the venison. *See back jacket image.*

3 lbs. ground venison (shoulder is best)

1 lb. ground pork

2 cups finely chopped fresh leeks (white & pale green parts only)

$^1/_2$ cup extra-virgin olive oil

Salt & freshly ground pepper

3 Tbsp. Hungarian (hot) paprika

$1^1/_2$ lbs. cleaned pork casings

In a large mixing bowl, combine all the ingredients except the casings. Work the mixture together well with your hands, kneading the oil, leeks and spices into the meat thoroughly. Taste the mixture by pinching off a small amount and frying it in a pan. Season with salt and pepper and additional paprika, if desired. When the mixture is to your liking, place the casings onto the sausage machine or food-processor attachment, add the meat and proceed according to the manufacturer's instructions. Sausages may be refrigerated up to 4 days or frozen up to 2 months. To cook, sausages may be emptied and crumbled into a frying pan, scored with a knife and pan-fried or, my favorite, grilled over a bed of hot coals on a warm summer day

Makes 4$^1/_4$ pounds of sausages, uncooked.

Magnotta selection: 1995 Cabernet Sauvignon Limited Edition

Bison Kabobs

These easy kabobs can be made with any large game meat. Simply prepare all the elements ahead of time, and all there is left to do is beat up the grill, set the picnic table and open a bottle of wine!

2-2$^1/_2$ lbs. bison shoulder, all silver skin removed *(see p. 94)*

1 recipe Marinade for Big Game *(see p. 5)*

$^1/_2$ cup olive oil

Juice of 2 lemons

2 Tbsp. chopped fresh oregano

Salt & freshly ground pepper

3 green peppers, seeds removed

3 medium onions, peeled

16 cherry tomatoes

16 firm white mushrooms

* long metal skewers

1 Cut the bison into 2″ cubes, and place in a shallow, nonreactive dish with the marinade. Stir to coat the meat thoroughly, and refrigerate 24 hours or overnight.

2 If planning to cook the kabobs right away, heat up the grill, barbecue or broiler to high. Remove the bison from the marinade, and place in a colander to drain. Transfer the meat to a bowl with olive oil, lemon juice, oregano and salt and pepper; toss together. Set aside for 15 to 20 minutes.

3 Cut the green peppers and onions into 1$^1/_2$″ square pieces. Assemble the kabobs by alternating the peppers, onions, cherry tomatoes, mushrooms and bison cubes along the metal skewers.

Repeat until all the ingredients are used, and transfer the finished skewers to a large shallow dish. Pour the lemon-olive oil mixture over them, and refrigerate until needed.

4 Wipe a lightly oiled cloth across the hot grill bars to prevent sticking, and wipe the excess marinade from the skewers. Grill each one for several minutes each side, or until desired doneness, basting once or twice with the lemon-olive oil mixture. Take care not to overcook; bison is ideal when rare to medium-rare. Serve with baked potatoes or rice and a hearty red wine.

Makes 6 to 8 servings.

Bison Salisbury Steak

While these delicious steaks are wonderful on their own, when sandwiched in a crusty roll, they elevate the common hamburger to new heights. Grinding tenderizes tougher meat, which is always the most flavorful. I guarantee this will be the best burger you've ever made! Venison and elk also benefit from being prepared this way.

2 lbs. ground bison shoulder (your butcher can do this for you)

$1/_3$ cup finely chopped onions

2 Tbsp. chopped fresh parsley (preferably Italian flat-leaf parsley), plus additional for garnish (optional)

2 cloves garlic, peeled & finely chopped

2 Tbsp. olive oil

Salt & freshly ground pepper

8-12 thick buns or slices of bread for grilling (optional)

Green onions for garnish

1 Preheat grill or frying pan (preferably cast iron) to medium-high to high. In a medium-size bowl, combine ground bison, onions, parsley, garlic and olive oil, and season well with salt and pepper. Knead ingredients together well with your hands, evenly distributing the seasonings. Form into $1/_2$" thick patties about 5" in diameter for steaks or $31/_2$" for burgers.

2 Wipe hot grill bars with a lightly oiled cloth to prevent sticking, and grill the steaks a few minutes on both sides, or until desired doneness. These steaks are best when served medium-rare. If desired, grill the bread before assembling the burgers. Garnish with fresh green onions and additional chopped parsley.

Makes 6 servings.

Magnotta selection: 1998 Carmenère Gran Riserva

Grilled Marinated Bison Steaks

Do grill these simple steaks — the smoky flavor accents the full, gamey taste of bison.

1 recipe Marinade for Big Game *(see p. 5)*

4 bison T-bone steaks, cut 1≤ thick

Salt & freshly ground pepper

1 Prepare the marinade, and place in a shallow, nonreactive dish. Add the bison steaks, turning to coat, and refrigerate 24 hours or overnight.

2 Heat up the grill, and allow to get very hot. Wipe the hot bars with a lightly oiled cloth to prevent sticking. Remove the steaks from the marinade, and wipe off excess. Season well with salt and pepper, and grill for a few minutes on both sides, or until desired doneness. I prefer to serve these flavorful steaks medium-rare. Sautéed green vegetables, baked potatoes and a lusty red wine are perfect accompaniments.

Makes 4 servings.

Magnotta selection: 1998 Carmenère Gran Riserva

Wine Buffalo Sausages

Wine-infused sausages are very popular in traditional cooking all over Greece. I have found that they are particularly good when made with big game, such as bison -the red wine balances the rich and assertive taste of the meat.

3 lbs. ground bison (buffalo), preferably shoulder

1 lb. ground pork

$1/_2$-$3/_4$ cup dry red wine

3 large onions, peeled & finely chopped

1 Tbsp. ground coriander

Salt & freshly ground pepper

1 tsp. cayenne pepper, or to taste

$1^1/_2$ lb. cleaned pork casings

1 Combine all of the ingredients except the casings in a large mixing bowl. Knead the mixture with your hands until thoroughly combined. To taste for seasoning, pinch off a small amount and fry it until cooked. Adjust salt and pepper and cayenne.

2 Place casings around the sausage maker, and proceed according to manufacturer's instructions. Sausages may be refrigerated up to 3 days or frozen up to 2 months. To cook, grill over a bed of hot coals or, alternatively, crumble the contents of the casings into a frying pan or score the sausages with a sharp knife and pan-fry.

Makes 4 pounds of sausages.

Braised Elk with Pasta

Thank heaven for cowboys! A good friend of mine, George Antonopoulos, is a skilled hunter and has the distinction of having shot seven elk in his lifetime. Some years ago, George and I were out on the range in Colorado together — he was hunting elk, and I was looking for game birds. We created this recipe with the elk, the simple ingredients we had on hand and a lot of laughter.

1 3-to-4-lb. boneless roast of elk (loin, leg or shoulder)

2 cloves garlic, peeled & slivered

$^1/_4$ cup olive oil

Salt & freshly ground pepper

1 cup beef stock, preferably homemade, or canned low-salt broth

1 cup dry red wine

1 bay leaf

1 lb. fresh pasta noodles, such as fettuccine

2-3 Tbsp. butter

2 Tbsp. chopped fresh parsley (preferably Italian flat-leaf)

$^1/_3$ cup freshly grated Parmesan cheese

1 Preheat oven to 375°F. Tie the meat securely so that it forms a fairly uniform cylinder. With the tip of a small, sharp knife, make evenly spaced slits in the meat. Insert garlic slivers into the holes, burying them deeply. In an ovenproof pan, heat olive oil over medium-high heat. Pat the meat dry, season with salt and pepper. Brown the meat on all sides, then add the beef stock. Bring to a boil, and deglaze the pan, scraping up any brown bits from the bottom. Add wine and bay leaf, and bake, covered, for 1 hour. Remove the cover, and baste elk with the pan juices. Return to the oven for another 45 minutes to 1 hour, basting frequently until an instant-read meat thermometer inserted in the center of the roast registers

125°. Transfer elk to a platter, cover with foil, and let rest for 5 to 20 minutes. Skim excess fat from the pan juices, and keep hot.

2 Meanwhile, bring a pot of salted water to a boil, add pasta, and cook until al dente. Drain and toss with butter and 1 tablespoon chopped parsley.

3 To serve, surround elk roast with pasta. Pour it pan juices over pasta, and garnish with grated Parmesan and remaining chopped parsley.

Makes 6 to 8 servings.

Magnotta selection: 1999 Maréchal Foch Barrel Aged

Elk Game Pie

This French-inspired pie is an exquisite main course for an elegant dinner party. The prepared pie can be frozen, tightly wrapped, up to 1 month. To serve, simply place the frozen pie into the preheated oven and allow an extra 1/2-hour baking time.

2 Tbsp. olive oil

3 lbs. ground elk (such as shoulder or eye of round)

2 medium onions, peeled & finely chopped

2 celery stalks, chopped in $^1/_8''$ pieces

1 cup milk (not low-fat)

1 10-oz. can condensed cream of mushroom soup

Salt & freshly ground pepper

French Lining Pastry:

4 cups all-purpose flour

1 tsp. salt

$1^1/_4$ cups butter, chilled & cut into small cubes

2 eggs

$1^3/_4$ cups cold water

1 Tbsp. olive oil

1 For pastry: Sift flour and salt into a large bowl. Add butter, and use a pastry cutter or two knives to cut it into flour until the mixture looks like coarse oatmeal. In a small bowl, whisk together 1 egg and water, then add mixture all at once to the flour-butter meal. With your hand, gently and quickly blend the ingredients together until the dough forms a large ball. Divide into 2 portions: $^1/_3$ and $^2/_3$. Form each portion into a ball, and flatten into a disk. Wrap disks securely in plastic wrap, and refrigerate for at least 1 hour.

2 For filling: In a large skillet, heat the olive oil over medium-high heat. Add the ground elk, and sauté until browned but not completely cooked. With a slotted spoon, transfer elk to a large bowl, and pour off the excess fat from the skillet. Reduce heat to medium, and add onions and celery. Stir just until browned in the juices, and add to the elk, along with the milk, mushroom soup and salt and pepper to taste. Mix well, and set aside to cool.

3 Remove dough from refrigerator, and on a lightly floured surface, roll out the larger portion to $1/4''$ thick. Line the bottom and sides of a 9'' springform pan, carefully pressing dough in to seal the seam where they meet. Leave a 1'' overhang. Spoon the cooled elk mixture into the pan, keeping the rim of dough clean. Beat the remaining egg together with the tablespoon olive oil, and brush the rim with this egg wash. Roll out the other piece of dough, and lay over the filling in the pan. Press edges of dough together, and trim the overhang. Brush the top of the pie with egg wash, and use a small, sharp knife to make three of four slits to allow steam to escape. Refrigerate 15 minutes.

4 Preheat oven to 400°F. Place the pie on a baking sheet to catch any leaks, and set on the middle rack of the oven. Bake for 15 minutes, then reduce heat to 350°. Continue baking about 1 hour, or until crust is golden brown and the tip of a skewer inserted through one of the slits feels hot when touched to your lower lip. Allow pie to cool slightly, then carefully remove sides of pan, and serve warm. This pie is wonderful with a homemade relish or chutney.

Makes 8 servings.

Braised Antelope Chops

This dish was my first experience at the table with antelope. I was hunting on the grassy plains of southern Saskatchewan, and a good friend of mine, a chef, made these fabulous chops for me. They now hold a permanent place of honor at all the special-event dinners that I hold each year.

12-18 small new potatoes, depending on size

6 antelope loin chops

Salt & freshly ground pepper

3 Tbsp. butter

$1^1/_2$ Tbsp. Worcestershire sauce

$^1/_4$ cup water or beef stock

6 firm, ripe tomatoes, halved

1 Tbsp. chopped fresh oregano

Fresh watercress sprigs for garnish

1 Cover potatoes with water in a medium pot. Bring to a boll, and cook until just tender but slightly undercooked. Drain, cool, cut in half, and reserve.

2 Wash antelope chops, pat dry, and season well with salt and pepper. In a heavy, preferably cast-iron skillet, heat 1 tablespoon butter, $^1/_2$ tablespoon Worcestershire sauce and $^1/_4$ cup water or beef stock over medium-high heat. Add 2 chops, and cook to desired doneness; repeat with remaining butter, Worcestershire sauce and chops. Remove chops to a warm platter.

3 Drain off excess fat from the skillet, then add tomatoes, potatoes and oregano, and sauté over medium heat until well flavored and potatoes begin to brown. Season to taste with salt and pepper. Serve immediately, with antelope chops surrounded by tomatoes and potatoes. Garnish with watercress.

Makes 6 servings.

Magnotta selection: 1998 Merlot Gran Riserva

Carbonnade à la Flamande of Wild Boar

Carbonnade is a rich, thick beef stew in the style of Flanders, made with onions, often bacon and strong Belgian beer. In this variation, wild boar replaces both the beef and the bacon and produces a hugely flavorful dish. Centuries ago, the original carbonnade may have even been made with the European wild boar-a meat much more common and less valuable than the cow. Do try to get a dark Belgian or German beer for this recipe; if that is impossible, substitute another dark, rich Belgian-style ale. This recipe may be halved.

4 cups beef stock, preferably homemade, or canned low-salt broth

3 large leeks (white & pale green part only)

5 lbs. boneless wild boar meat (shoulder, loin, leg or any combination)

Salt & freshly ground pepper

2-3 cups flour

$1/4$ cup vegetable oil

$1^1/_2$ cups finely chopped onions

2 12-oz. bottles strong Belgian or German beer

1 Place beef stock in a small saucepan, and bring to a boil. Boil until reduced to $^3/_4$ cup. Reserve.

2 To clean leeks, slice them each lengthwise down the center, then slice each half in thin semicircles. Place the slices in a large basin of cool water, and swirl around with your hands. Carefully lift the leeks out of the water; the dirt will have sunk to the bottom of the basin. Dry the leeks with several layers of paper towel, and reserve.

3 Preheat oven to 375°F. Cut the boar meat into 2″ cubes, and season with salt and pepper. Place flour in a strong plastic bag, add boar cubes, and shake to coat thoroughly. Remove the meat, and shake off excess flour. Heat the vegetable oil in a large skillet over medium-high heat, and sauté the boar meat in batches until well browned. Remove from the skillet, and set aside.

Magnotta selection: Ducks Unlimited 2000 Cabernet Franc VQA

4 Drain the excess fat from the skillet, and add leeks and onions. Sauté over medium-low heat until softened and beginning to brown. Arrange half of the leek-onion mixture in the bottom of a deep casserole. Add half the wild boar pieces, then another layer of leeks and onions. Top with the rest of the meat. Pour 1 bottle of beer into the skillet, and bring to a boil, scraping up any brown bits from the bottom. Transfer the contents of the skillet to the casserole, and add the other bottle of beer and the beef stock. Cover the casserole, and bake for 2 hours, or until boar is very tender and sauce is thickened. Taste and adjust seasoning with salt and pepper. Serve with mashed potatoes or buttered egg noodles.

Makes 10 to 12 servings.

Wild Boar Sausages with Orange

In the south of Greece, homemade sausages are often accented by the sparkling zest of fresh orange rind. This recipe is from Pelaponnisos, where my family comes from.

3 lbs. ground wild boar

1 lb. ground pork

Juice of 3 oranges

Zest of 1-2 oranges, finely chopped

Salt & freshly ground pepper

1½ lbs. cleaned pork casings

1 In a large mixing bowl, combine boar, pork, orange juice and zest of 1 orange, and season well with salt and pepper. With your hands, knead the mixture together to thoroughly incorporate the seasonings. To taste, pinch off a small amount of the meat and pan-fry it. Adjust seasoning with salt, pepper and additional orange zest.

2 When the mixture is to your liking, place casings on the sausage machine and proceed according to manufacturer's instructions. The best way to cook these is over a bed of hot coals, but they may also be scored with a sharp knife and pan-fried or emptied, crumbled and sautéed. Serve with sweet or hot mustard on the side.

Makes 4 pounds of sausages.

Medallions of Wild Boar with Port

This dish makes a luxurious entrée for a special dinner — the sweet richness of the port pairs beautifully with the gaminess of the wild boar.

1½ lbs. wild boar tenderloin, trimmed of all silver skin *(see p. 94)*

Salt & freshly ground pepper

2 Tbsp. butter

2 Tbsp. olive oil

6-8 firm white mushrooms, sliced

1 large onion, peeled & finely chopped

½ cup port

1 With a long slicing knife, slice the tenderloin across the grain into 1"-thick medallions. Season well with salt and pepper. In a large skillet, heat butter and oil over medium-high heat. Working in batches, add the medallions of boar, and brown for 2 to 3 minutes on each side. Remove from the skillet, and pour off the excess fat.

2 Add the mushrooms, and sauté over high heat until they are brown and all the liquid has evaporated. Remove and reduce the heat under the pan to medium-low. Add the onions, and sweat until they are soft and beginning to color. Return the mushrooms and medallions of boar to the skillet, and add the port. Bring to a boil, and reduce, scraping up any brown bits from the bottom. Simmer for 5 to 6 minutes, or until boar is tender and port is reduced to a glaze. Serve medallions with a spoonful of the glaze over top, with roast potatoes and steamed vegetables.

Makes 4 to 6 servings.

Ostrich Pot Roast

Ostrich is a rich and very meaty bird, now being raised on many farms across North America. It is much closer to pork or veal in texture than it is to chicken or turkey and benefits greatly from hearty preparations such as this warming pot roast.

1 4-to-5-lb. ostrich roast

Salt & freshly ground pepper

$1/4$ cup olive oil

3 large onions, peeled & thinly sliced

1 clove garlic, peeled & crushed

$1/2$ cup dry red wine, preferably Burgundy

2 cups very hot chamomile tea

16 pitted prunes

12 Kalamata olives

5 large mushrooms, sliced

1 Tbsp. cornstarch

1 Preheat oven to 325°F. Trim the roast, and remove any silver skin *(see page 94)*. Truss the roast so that it is a uniform cylinder, and season well with salt and pepper. Heat olive oil in a large Dutch oven over low heat, and add onions and garlic. Sauté until onions are soft and translucent. Add the roast to the pot, and pour red wine over. Cover and bake for 2 hours.

2 Meanwhile, pour chamomile tea over the prunes in a medium-size nonreactive bowl, and allow prunes to plump. After 2 hours, strain the prunes, reserving $3/4$ cup of the liquid. Add the prunes, the liquid, olives and mushrooms to the roast, and cover again. Return pot to the oven, and continue cooking for another 1 to $1^1/2$ hours, or until roast is tender and registers between 160° and 180° on an instant-read meat thermometer inserted at the thickest point. A temperature of 160° will produce a rare roast, 170° a medium roast, 180° a well-done roast. Allow the roast to rest for 15 minutes before carving.

3 Meanwhile, skim any fat from the juices in the pot. Combine cornstarch with a small amount of water, and stir to make a smooth paste. Remove pot from the heat, whisk cornstarch paste into the cooking liquid, and return pot to heat. Whisking constantly, bring the liquid to a boil over medium-high heat until sauce thickens. Transfer to a warmed sauceboat, and serve with the ostrich roast.

Makes 6 to 8 servings.

❧ My Favorite Game Fish ❧

Few things in these modern times can draw us closer to our roots than pulling a silvery fish from the cold, clear water of a stream and cooking it quickly and simply with flavors that don't mask its delicious sweetness! While I admit that fish don't traditionally fall into the category of wild game, I also confess to being in love with sportfishing, and a section on fish seemed to me a natural addition to this book. The range of fish available to the amateur angler in North America is vast, but one group that is as attractive to the gourmet as to the sportsman is the trout and salmon family. These beautiful fish are among my favorites to catch and to eat! Through the centuries, the family of fish that includes trout, salmon and arctic char has become prized for its flavorful flesh — Napoleon, a passionate gourmet, enjoyed eating trout caught out of the rushing streams of the Alps.

Members of this family of fish, known as salmonids, are extremely sensitive to pollutants and thus are environmental barometers for the level of pollutants in source water. Unfortunately, because of acid rain and poor agricultural practices, they are becoming increasingly rare in the wild; but salmonids are being very ably farmed all over the world. If you are lucky enough to know a natural location where these species thrive, you can be certain it is pure, unpolluted water.

Fish, like many species of wild game, are enjoying a new popularity in today's lighter cuisine. Besides being low in harmful fats and high in celebrated Omega-3 fatty acids, they are an excellent source of protein, iron and B vitamins.

Rainbow trout, brook or speckled trout, salmon and brown trout are perhaps the most preferred trout by culinary standards. Although there are differences in nuances of flavor, all trout are rich, fine-textured fish. The flesh of wild trout has a complex, delicate flavor and may be white, pink, light orange or quite red in color. Farmed fish are slightly less complex in taste and are usually paler and less vibrantly colored than their wild counterparts.

Salmon varies greatly in taste, size and composition, depending on the variety and whether it is wild or farmed. Some species of wild salmon can reach 120 pounds, but for ease of cooking, look for a whole salmon that is about 5 to 8 pounds. Like trout, salmon are a fatty species, a characteristic that gives them their deep, rich flavor. Wild salmon are bright pink or tangerine-colored, while farm-raised salmon, though raised in salt water, are somewhat more muted, in both flavor and color.

I have shared some of my favorite recipes for these noble species, including a recipe for the majestic arctic char and one for fried bass that my family adores! Always try to buy the freshest fish possible — it will make all the difference in the world to the finished dish.

Spanish Mountain Trout

Napoleon Bonaparte had an affinity for many good things (and some not so good!), one of which was eating the sweet trout caught in the cold streams of the Spanish mountains. This is my own modification of a recipe I once read that was reputed to be one of his favorites.

2 ripe tomatoes, such as beefsteak or plum

4 10-oz. trout, cleaned

Salt & freshly ground pepper

1 Tbsp. butter

$1/4$ cup fruity olive oil

1 clove garlic, peeled & finely chopped

$1/4$ cup freshly grated Romano or Parmesan cheese

2 Tbsp. freshly chopped parsley for garnish

1 To peel and seed tomatoes: Bring a small pot of water to a boll. With a sharp paring knife, cut out the stem scar, and score the smooth end of the tomato with a small "x." Drop the tomatoes carefully into the water, and boll for 30 seconds to 1 minute, depending on the ripeness. Remove and plunge the tomatoes into a waiting bowl of ice water to stop the cooking. When the tomatoes are cool, the skins will peel off easily. To remove seeds, cut the tomatoes in half across the axis (horizontally). Either squeeze the halves, letting the seeds fall out, or use a teaspoon to scoop them out. Chop the flesh into small cubes.

2 Wash the trout, pat dry, and season with salt and pepper inside and out. In a large skillet, preferably cast iron, heat the butter and 2 tablespoons of the oil over medium-high heat. Place the trout in the skillet, and cook on each side for about 2 minutes, or until browned.

3 Meanwhile, in a medium saucepan, heat the remaining oil over high heat. When the oil is hot but not smoking, add the chopped tomatoes and let sit for a moment before shaking the pan. Allow the heat to release the juice from the tomatoes and form an emulsion between the juice and the oil. Reduce heat slightly, and cook until tomatoes begin to break down, about 3 minutes. Transfer the tomato-oil mixture to the skillet with the fish, and add garlic. Sprinkle with Romano or Parmesan cheese, reduce heat to medium-low, and cover the pan for 2 minutes to melt the cheese. Arrange trout on a platter, top with tomatoes, and sprinkle with chopped parsley. Serve with rice or roast potatoes.

Makes 4 servings.

Magnotta selection: 1996 Gewürztraminer Dry Limited Edition

Brown Trout à la George

I call myself the Bay Leaf King. Quite by accident one day, while on a hunting trip with no other seasonings, I discovered the sincerely underappreciated value of the humble bay leaf. Since then, I have used it extensively in many dishes, often as a primary flavor. Bay has a floral, earthy taste that complements the delicate sweetness of these simply prepared fish. Serve this dish with lemon wedges and extra freshly ground pepper.

4 10-oz. brown (or other) trout, cleaned

Salt & freshly ground pepper

2 Tbsp. butter

3 Tbsp. olive oil

1 bay leaf

$1/4$ cup dry white wine

1 Wash the trout, pat dry, and season well inside and out with salt and pepper. In a large skillet, heat the butter and olive oil over medium-low heat, and add the bay leaf. Reducing the heat, if necessary, let the bay leaf infuse the butter-oil mixture for 5 minutes. Remove the bay leaf, and discard.

2 Raise the heat to medium-high, and when the oil Is hot, add the trout. Cook each side for 1 to 2 minutes, or until skin is crisp and brown. Add the wine, and partially cover. Simmer for 2 minutes, or until flesh is opaque. Serve immediately, pouring the pan juices over the fish.

Makes 4 servings.

Rainbow Trout with Lemon and Wine

The lemon juice and white wine conspire to give a refreshing brightness to this lovely fish. Perhaps surprisingly, this dish goes beautifully with French-fried potatoes and a dry white wine.

4 10-oz. rainbow (or other) trout, cleaned

Salt & freshly ground pepper

2 cups all-purpose flour

2 Tbsp. butter

1 Tbsp. olive oil

Juice of 1 lemon

$^1/_2$ cup dry white wine

1 Season the trout inside and out with salt and pepper. Place the flour in a strong plastic bag. Add the trout one at a time, shaking to coat thoroughly. Shake off excess flour.

2 In a large skillet, heat the butter and oil over medium-high heat. When the foam subsides, add the trout and sauté each side for 1 to 2 minutes, or until skin is golden. Add lemon juice, and simmer for 2 minutes. Add wine, cover, and simmer for 2 to 3 minutes, or until trout flesh is opaque. Remove to a warmed platter, and pour pan juices over fish.

Makes 4 servings.

Trout Amandine

When I fly-fish in a trout stream, I am concentrating on catching the elusive fish. While I am driving home after a successful trip, my thoughts are already imagining the sweet rich aroma of sizzling trout with almonds, and it is all I can do to stay focused on the road!

4 10-oz. trout, cleaned

Salt & freshly ground pepper

2 cups all-purpose flour

1 Tbsp. chopped fresh thyme

1 Tbsp. chopped fresh rosemary

5 Tbsp. butter

$1/3$ cup sliced or slivered blanched almonds, as fresh as possible

1 Season trout with salt and pepper inside and out. Combine flour and herbs in a strong plastic bag, and add trout one by one, shaking to coat. Shake off excess flour.

2 In a large skillet, heat 3 tablespoons butter over medium-high heat. When foam subsides, add trout and sauté each side for 2 to 3 minutes, or until skin is crisp and golden and flesh is opaque.

3 In a smaller skillet or saucepan, heat remaining butter over medium-low heat, and add the almonds. Sauté, shaking frequently, until the butter and almonds begin to brown. Watch closely, and remove the pan from the heat just as the color starts to change, because almonds burn very quickly; the residual heat will deepen the color.

4 Arrange the trout on a warmed platter, and top with the almond-butter mixture.

Makes 4 servings.

Magnotta selection: 1999 Pinot Gris VQA

Steamed Arctic Char

Arctic char is closely related to both the trout and the salmon. They reside in the icy waters of arctic streams but are becoming more readily available to the average consumer since farms in Iceland are now raising them. Char has a wonderful flavor and texture that is somewhere between that of salmon and trout.

$1/4$ cup + 2 Tbsp. butter

4 12-to-16-oz. arctic char cleaned & scaled

Salt & freshly ground pepper

1 large onion, peeled & thinly sliced

6 Tbsp. freshly chopped parsley (preferably Italian flat-leaf)

$1/4$ cup dry white wine (optional)

12 small new potatoes

4 large sheets of extra-strong aluminum foil

1 Preheat oven to 375°F. Smear each sheet of foil with 1 tablespoon of butter, leaving a thick film. Wash the char, pat dry, and season well with salt and pepper inside and out. Place a char on one end of each sheet of foil, and stuff each cavity with overlapping slices of onion and 1 tablespoon parsley. Sprinkle 1 tablespoon of wine over each fish. Bring the end of the foil up over the char, folding the edges together tightly to seal the seams. (Recipe may be completed up to this point and refrigerated up to 4 hours. Allow fish to come to room temperature before proceeding with baking.)

2 Place the foil packets on a baking sheet, and bake for 20 to 30 minutes, depending on thickness of fish.

3. Meanwhile, boil the potatoes in a pot of well-salted water until tender. Drain and toss with 2 tablespoons butter and remaining parsley. Bring the sealed packets to the table, and allow diners to open them themselves. Take care to avoid the rush of steam that will escape when the packets are first opened. Serve with the herbed new potatoes.

Makes 4 servings.

Magnotta selection: 1996 Sauvignon Blanc Limited Edition

Pan-Fried Bass with Curried Rice

I came up with this unusual recipe while at the cottage with my family. Bass fishing is very good there, and we were all becoming a little tired of my usual recipes, so I got creative one night — my children love it.

1 2-to-3-lb. large freshwater bass or sunfish, cleaned & scaled

Juice of 1 lemon

1 cup long-grain rice, rinsed well

1 cup water

$1/4$ cup butter

3 Tbsp. curry powder

Salt & freshly ground pepper

2 Tbsp. olive oil

3 Tbsp. finely chopped fresh chives for garnish

1 With a sharp filleting knife, remove the two fillets as cleanly as possible from the bass, leaving the head, backbone and tall intact (your fishmonger may do this for you). Remove the skin by placing the fillet, skin side down, on a cutting surface and working the thin blade of the knife on an angle across the skin in between it and the flesh. Remove any small pin bones with a pair of needle-nosed pliers. Cut the bass fillets into 2″ cubes, and combine in a nonreactive bowl with the lemon juice. Stir to coat thoroughly, and marinate for 15 minutes.

2 Meanwhile, combine rice and water in a small saucepan, bring to a boll, and simmer 20 minutes, or until rice is tender and all the water has been absorbed. In a separate saucepan, melt 2 tablespoons of the butter over medium heat, and add the curry powder. Stir constantly for 2 minutes until fragrant and warm. Add the rice, stir to coat well, and season with salt and pepper. Keep warm.

3 After the fish has been marinating for 15 minutes, transfer to a colander and allow to drain for a minute or so. Season with salt and pepper. Heat the oil and remaining 2 tablespoons of the butter together in a large skillet over medium-high heat. When the foam subsides, add the fish, and sauté, turning to brown evenly, until pieces are golden and flesh is firm and flakes easily. Mound the curried rice on a warm platter, and arrange the fried bass on top. Garnish with chopped chives, and serve with lemon wedges.

Makes 5 to 4 servings.

Magnotta selection: 1998 Riesling Medium Dry VQA

Salmon Steak in Garlic Butter

One summer evening, I was invited to dine with my brother-in-law. Kostas is a very skilled computer-software expert but, in my experience, not much of a cook. To my surprise, he introduced me to this wonderful dish, and I have enjoyed it many times since.

$^1/_4$ cup butter

4 garlic cloves, peeled & finely chopped

4 center-cut salmon steaks, about 1≤ thick

Salt & freshly ground pepper

1 Tbsp. olive oil

3 Tbsp. freshly chopped parsley (preferably Italian flat-leaf) for garnish

1 In a small saucepan, heat butter and garlic together over low heat. Stir occasionally, and let the garlic infuse the butter for about 5 minutes. Remove from heat, and strain, discarding the garlic. Wash the salmon steaks, pat dry, season with salt and pepper, and brush on each side with the garlic butter. Let stand for 10 to 15 minutes.

2 In a large skillet, heat the remaining garlic butter with olive oil over medium-high heat. Add the salmon steaks, and cook each side for 4 to 5 minutes, or until the flesh is golden and firm. Transfer the steaks to a warmed platter, pour the pan juices over the fish, and sprinkle with the chopped parsley.

Makes 4 servings.

Magnotta selection: 1997 Chardonnay Barrel Fermented VQA

Pan-Fried Brook Trout

This is a somewhat more elegant version of the dish I had for my first shore lunch on a fishing trip at the age of 12. On these trips, my uncles and brother-in-law would always bring along a small skillet, a bag of seasoned flour, a little butter or oil and maybe a few fresh herbs. We pulled the fish out of the clear, cold water, cleaned them and sautéed them over a little fire in the butter and herbs. To this day, my mouth waters as I remember how succulent and sweet those trout were! As with any fish dish, success lies in the freshness of the fish — while you may not be cooking on the shores of a babbling brook, do use the freshest fish you can find.

2 cups all-purpose flour

1 Tbsp. chopped fresh thyme

1 Tbsp. chopped fresh rosemary

4 10-oz. brook (or other) trout, cleaned

Salt & freshly ground pepper

3 Tbsp. butter

2 Tbsp. olive oil

$^1/_4$ cup brandy

Lemon wedges for garnish

Tbsp. chopped fresh parsley (preferably Italian flat-leaf) for garnish

Combine flour, thyme and rosemary in a strong plastic bag. Season the trout well inside and out with salt and pepper. Shake each trout in the herbed flour, then remove, and shake off excess. In a large skillet, heat the butter and oil together over medium-high heat. When the foam begins to subside, add the trout, and brown each side for 1 to 2 minutes, until skin is brown and crisp. Add the brandy, and cover the skillet. Cook another 5 to 6 minutes, uncover, and continue cooking until the flesh is opaque. Pour the hot pan juices over the fish, and garnish with lemon wedges and chopped fresh parsley.

Makes 4 servings.

Whole Salmon Baked in Foil

Baking fish in a foil packet allows it to retain all its natural juices and flavor. The fish actually steams inside the foil and comes out delicate, moist and succulent. Any fish may be cooked this way, whole or in steaks or fillets. The packet may be completely prepared and sealed ahead of time and simply brought to room temperature before baking. The packet makes a dramatic presentation when opened at the table in front of guests, but take care not to burn yourself on the rush of steam that will escape.

2 Tbsp. butter

1 whole 3-to-5lb. salmon, cleaned & scaled

Salt & freshly ground pepper

2 lemons, thinly sliced, seeds removed

1 large or 2 small onions, peeled & thinly sliced

1 Tbsp. chopped fresh oregano

2 Tbsp. olive oil

$^1/_4$ cup dry white wine

One sheet of extra-strong aluminum foil, about $2^1/_2$ times the length of the salmon

1 Preheat oven to 375°F. Smear one side of the foil with the butter, leaving a thick film. Wash the salmon, pat dry, and season well with salt and pepper inside and out. Lay the salmon on one end of the foil, and stuff the cavity with overlapping slices of lemon and onion. Sprinkle this stuffing with half of the oregano. Rub the skin with the olive oil, and pour the wine over the fish, cupping the foil at the edges to avoid spilling the liquid. Sprinkle the skin with the remaining oregano, and fold the other half of the foil sheet up over the salmon. Seal the three edges tightly to avoid any leaks. (Salmon may be prepared up to this point and refrigerated up to 4 hours. Allow fish to return to room temperature before baking.)

2 Place packet on a baking sheet, and bake for 35 to 45 minutes, depending on the thickness of the fish. Present packet at the table, and open in front of guests. Serve with rice and glazed vegetables.

Makes 4 to 6 servings.

Selected Wine List

1999 Vidal Limited Edition Icewine

Unlimited 1999 Viognier VQA

1998 Blanc Fume' Gran Riserva

1999 Assemblage VQA (a blend of Riesling, Pinot Gris and Gewürztraminer)

1999 Zweigelt-Merlot VQA

1999 Pinot Noir Special Reserve

1999 Cab Franc Merlot VQA

1999 Chardonnay Barrel Aged VQA

1999 Pinot Noir VQA

1999 Chardonnay Merritt Road VQA

1996 Viognier Limited Edition

1999 Cabernet Franc Limited Edition VQA

1998 Pinot Gris Special Reserve

1999 Cabernet Sauvignon VQA

1995 Merlot Limited Edition

1998 Cabernet Sauvignon Special Reserve

1999 Meritage VQA (a blend of Cabernet Sauvignon, Cabernet Franc and Merlot)

1996 Magnotta Millennium (Cabernet Sauvignon)

1995 Cabernet Merlot Limited Edition

1998 II Cacciatore (a blend of Cabernet Sauvignon, Merlot and Carmenère)

1999 Merlot VQA

1998 Carmenère Gran Riserva

1999 Maréchal Foch Barrel Aged

1998 Merlot Gran Riserva

Ducks Unlimited 2000 Cabernet Franc VQA

1996 Gewürztraminer Dry Limited Edition

1999 Pinot Gris VQA

1996 Sauvignon Blanc Limited Edition

1998 Riesling Medium Dry VQA

1997 Chardonnay Barrel Fermented VQA

Selected Suppliers of Game

Canada

Lakeland Game Meats

1226 St. Paul Street West
St. Catharines, Ontario
L2R 6P7
(905) 688-4570
1-800-665-3547
Mail order in Ontario only.
Pheasant, quail, guinea fowl, partridge, venison, bison, wild boar.

Lonnie Cowan

R.R. #1
Vittoria, Ontario
N0E 1W0
(519) 426-7302
Pick-up only.
Venison.

Pusateri's Fine Foods

1539 Avenue Road
Toronto, Ontario
M5M 3X4
(416) 785-9100
Delivery within Toronto or pick-up.
Pheasant, quail, guinea fowl, rabbit, venison, wild boar, salmon,
    trout, arctic char.

Mary Richmond

St. Lawrence Market
92 Front Street East
Toronto, Ontario
M5E 1C4
(519) 428-1230
Pick-up only.
Pheasant, quail, guinea fowl, partridge, turkey, venison, bison,
    wild boar.

United Stated of America

D'Artagnan Inc., Game Suppliers

280 Wilson Avenue
Newark, New Jersey
07105
(973) 344-0565 / 1-800-327-8246
Mail order within USA only.
Game birds, duck, foie gras, smoked fowl, big game,
    plus an extensive directory of specialty game products.

Game Sales International Inc.

P.O. Box 7719
Loveland, Colorado
80537-0719
1-800-729-2090
Mail order within USA only.
Pheasant, guinea fowl, quail, ostrich, mallard duck, foie gras,
    rabbit, red deer, kangaroo, alligator, New Zealand wapiti
    (elk), fallow deer, caribou, wild boar, rattlesnake, snapping
    turtle, plus many other species of fowl and big game.

Polarica/The Game Exchange

105 Quint Street
P.O. Box 880204
San Francisco, California
94124
(415) 647-1300
Mail order within the USA only.
Pheasant, guinea fowl, quail, all types of duck, squab,
    wild turkey, ostrich, emu, rabbit; an extensive selection of
    big game, including buffalo, antelope, venison, wild boar,
    Australian lamb, Holland veal. A wide variety of smoked
    products, including salmon, sturgeon and fowl.

Williams − Sonoma Inc.

P.O. BOX 7456
San Francisco, California
94120-7456
(800) 541-2233
U.S.A. Only

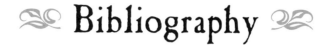

Bibliography

Anderson, Jean. *The Nutrition Bible*. New York, NY:
William Morrow and Co., © 1995.

Ash, John, and Sid Goldstein. *American Game Cooking*. New York, NY:
Addison-Wesley Publishing Co., © 1991.

Aspler, Tony. *Wine Lover's Companion*. Whitby, Ontario: McGraw-Hill Ryerson, © 1991.

Cole, Charles. *Gamebirds*. Limpsfield, Surrey, UK: Dragon's World Ltd., © 1983.

Cox, Jill, and Tony Lord. *Which Wine, Which Food*. London, UK: Mitchell Beazley, © 1994.

Hazen, Janet. *New Game Cuisine*. San Francisco, CA: Chronicle Books, © 1990.

Herbst, Sharon Tyler. *The New Food Lover's Companion*. Hauppauge, NY:
Barron's Educational Series Inc., © 1995.

Johnson, Hugh. *Pocket Guide to Wine 1996*. New York, NY:
Fireside Simon and Schuster Inc., © 1995.

Marrone, Teresa, et al. *Dressing and Cooking Wild Game*. Minnetonka, MN: Cy DeCosse Inc., ©
1987.

Pennington, Jean A.T. *Food Values of Portions Commonly Used, 15th ed.* New York, NY:
Harper Collins Publishers, © 1989.

Spier, Carol. *Food Essentials: Poultry*. New York, NY: Friedman Group, © 1993.

USDA. *Composition of Foods: Raw, Processed, Prepared*. Washington, DC:
© USDA, 1976-1993

Metric Equivalent Conversion Table

If you cook using metric measurements, here is a convenient way to convert imperial measurement to metric, using the Approximate Metric Equivalent system. The Approximate Metric Equivalent system works well, as long as you are consistent and apply it to every ingredient. Never mix two systems: whichever of the three systems below you choose to use, make sure you convert all of the ingredients to that system.

Imperial	Metric	Approximate Metric Equivalent
Conversion of Liquid Measures		
1/4 teaspoon	1.23 milliliters	
1/2 tsp.	2.46 mL	2.5 mL
3/4 tsp.	3.7 mL	
1 tsp.	4.93 mL	5 mL
1 1/2 tsp.	7.39 mL	
2 tsp.	9.86 mL	10 mL
1 tablespoon	14.79 mL	15 mL
2 tbsp.	29.57 mL	25 mL
1/4 cup	59.15 mL	60 mL
1/2 c.	118 mL	125 mL
1 c.	237 mL	250 mL
2 c.	473 mL	500 mL
3 c.	710 mL	750 mL
4c., 1 quart	946 mL	1 liter
Conversion of Solid Measures		
1 ounce	28.35 grams	30 g
4 oz.	113 g	125 g
8 oz.	226 g	250 g
16 oz., 1 pound	453 g	450 g
2 lbs.	906 g	900 g
2 1/4 lbs.	1.11 kg	1 kilogram
4 1/2 lbs.	2.04 kg	2 kg

Index